MICHAEL NELSON'S OTHER B

Queen Victoria and the Discovery of the Riviera (I.B. Tauris, 2001).

Of all the huge outpouring of Victoriana commemorating last month's centenary of the Queen-Empress's death, the most delightful study is this short and very well researched book by the former General Manager of Reuters, Michael Nelson.

It investigates the fully reciprocated love affair between the Queen and the French Riviera: she loved the South of France because of the climate, gardens and relative privacy; it loved her because of the prestige, publicity and tourism that her nine visits engendered.

Andrew Roberts in *The Sunday Telegraph*

One of the most fascinating books of the year ... Queen Vic helped invent international tourism – Britain's gift to the world.

Peter Preston in *The Guardian*

There is no lack of diverting sidelights. On her first visit, the Queen's train lacked a restaurant car, and she brought some of the food from Windsor, rather like a tripper taking sandwiches to Paris.

E.S. Turner in *The Times Literary Supplement*

Vastly researched and highly entertaining. She enjoyed the fireworks, laughed at the local newspapers, and tootled about in a donkey cart.

Unwisely, she entertained King Leopold of the Belgians, a paedophile who spent £800 a month on little English virgins and wore his fingernails so long that he daren't shake hands.

Brian Case in *Time Out*

Americans and the Making of the Riviera (McFarland, 2008).

Mr Nelson, well-known for his excellent book, *Queen Victoria and the Discovery of the Riviera*, here reminds us that Thomas Jefferson visited what became known as the Riviera in the late eighteenth century when the first English patients were going there for their consumption.

This is an enjoyable book that reminds us of the role America played in the development of this distinctive and largely pleasant part of France.

Contemporary Review

Nelson has had his head in a lot of books (and his walking boots on) and offers a fascinating account of this aspect of the Riviera's past.

This is a plumcake of a book, full of tasty morsels.

Patrick Middleton in *The Riviera Reporter*

This is an entertaining book about a niche subject, a light way of gathering further intelligence on great American writers and artists with a Francophile penchant.

Sylvie Wheatley in *France*

Americans were one of the most influential groups in the shaping of tourism on the Riviera in the 20th century, yet their achievements for the economy in the south of France are little documented.

Let's Go Riviera

The 'beautiful people' who gave the Riviera much of its glamour in the heady days before the '29 Wall Street crash – and left their names on dozens of Riviera streets and squares – are all here; millionaires, heiresses, impecunious geniuses who swam like a little shoal of fish among the rich.

Michael Taylor in *French News*

A History

Michael Nelson

Matador
9 Priory Business Park,
Wistow Road, Kibworth Beauchamp,
Leicestershire. LE8 0RX
Tel: 0116 279 2299
Email: books@troubador.co.uk
Web: www.troubador.co.uk/matador
Twitter: @matadorbooks

ISBN 978 1785898 334

British Library Cataloguing in Publication Data.
A catalogue record for this book is available from the British Library.

Typeset in 12pt Adobe Garamond Pro by Troubador Publishing Ltd, Leicester, UK

Matador is an imprint of Troubador Publishing Ltd

For Alba

Contents

List of Plates

Preface

When I was launching my *Americans and the Making of the Riviera* in Nice in 2008, Lin Wolff, owner of the English Book Centre in Valbonne, told me that customers were frequently coming into her shop and asking: "Do you have a general history of the Riviera in English?" She did not, because it did not exist. "Why don't you write one?" she said. So I did.

The Riviera was part of Provence for most of its history. Much of a history of the Riviera is therefore a history of Provence.

What is the Riviera today? The *Oxford English Dictionary* defines it as the name of the Italian seaboard about Genoa but that it is also applied to the Mediterranean coast from Marseilles in France to La Spezia in Italy. It quotes its first use in English as 1632, unrelated to France. The *Encyclopedia Britannica* is confused about its definition of the Riviera. At one point it says it is the Mediterranean coastland between Cannes (France) and La Spezia (Italy). In another entry it says it stretches from Marseilles to Pisa.

The Riviera lies in the departments of the Alpes-Maritimes, the Var and the Bouches-du-Rhône.

Stéphen Liégeard, who invented the term Côte d'Azur in his book of that name in 1887, put the western tip at Marseilles and the eastern at Genoa. He wanted his new name to replace the then current usage of Rivière and Riviéra and in the francophone world he succeeded.

In 1892 the publishers Murray produced a *Handbook to the Riviera, from Marseilles to Pisa*. In 1940 the French Blue Guides published *The Côte d'Azur from Marseilles to Menton*.

The *Michelin Green Guide* shows the Riviera stretching inland about 80 km or 50 miles at its maximum.

Queen Victoria first used the term Riviera in her journal on 12 April 1882 when she was in the train travelling between Cannes and Toulon on her way back to England after the first of her nine visits to the Riviera. She wrote: *"I must be grateful to have been permitted to spend 4 weeks in that lovely and far famed Riviera."*

A century earlier another visitor who was to become a head of state visited the Riviera. The visit in 1787 of Thomas Jefferson, who was to become the third president of the United States, has received little attention in either France or the United States. I was therefore pleased that the authorities of Nice named a street after him when I told them where he had stayed.

Introduction

The Riviera has been a sought-after territory for nearly 3,000 years. Throughout its history cosmopolitanism has been its overriding characteristic.

The first immigrants we can identify are the Greeks, fleeing from Turkey around 600 BC to escape the assaults of the Persians. Marseilles became the great *entrepôt* between Europe and the Levant. Then came the Romans because of the strategic position of the Riviera in the wars with Carthage.

The first time we meet the Riviera as a unit in history is between 536 and 558 AD when the Merovingian King Childebert ruled it, although it was not then called the Riviera. He governed from the Mediterranean coast south-west of Arles to just east of Nice.

In the seventh century Frankish kings, who had originated in Germany, set up a finishing school in Paris. Siagrius, the ruler of Provence, studied at the school and the son of King Edwin of Northumbria in England was also sent there.

Provence entered the most cosmopolitan rule in Europe in 1032 when it became part of what became known as the Holy Roman Empire. It was bequeathed as part of Burgundy to the German king and emperor Conrad II. After some tergiversations it left the empire when Provence was acquired by the Angevins in 1246. The title Holy Roman Empire was only invented in 1180 and not used much until 1254 after Provence had left. As the French philosopher Voltaire famously quipped, it was neither holy, nor Roman nor an empire.

In the Middle Ages the region was desired and fought for as a rich prize by Spain, Italy and France. It was a melting pot of juridical systems. Culturally, it produced the troubadours in the language of the Oc.

Provence did not fight in the Hundred Years' War between France and England and Burgundy, but – as so often in its history – it felt the repercussions of a neighbouring war. Armed bands, including Englishmen, left over from the war ravaged the Riviera.

France finally acquired Provence in the fifteenth century. As part of France, by the sixteenth it suffered the Wars of Religion and later the Frondes.

Given the importance of ecclesiastical institutions on the Riviera in the Middle Ages, it is surprising that it lacked any institutions of higher education. In 1500 there were universities in Valence, Orange, Avignon and Aix, but none in Marseilles or Nice.

A Provençal proverb says: *Lauso la mare e tente'n terro* (Praise the sea and stay on land). That respect for the sea is also shown by the Gulf of Lions, so named because the mistral wind roared like a lion. Peasants were nevertheless often also sailors for part of the year. But like their counterparts from other regions they tended to hug the shore. According to the galley accounts of a sixteenth-century Ragusan vessel it was a matter of buying one's butter at Villefranche, vinegar at Nice and oil and bacon at Toulon. The ships were like travelling bazaars. Tolls were not only levied by ports providing services, but also often by landowners which the ships passed by.

Over the span of Riviera history, the crops the peasants cultivated varied by demand and market conditions. They ranged from vines to wheat, oats, olives, lentils and peas.

The international character of the Riviera came into its own again in the second half of the eighteenth century when tourism started, mainly by the British in the winter. One of the earliest tourists was an American, Thomas Jefferson, minister in Paris and eventually to be the third President. His visit has been little written about in the United States or France, although he wrote many letters, which we have today because he brought with him a portable copying machine.

In the nineteenth century, the Russians and British were the predominant tourists. Monarchs were important in setting an example to their citizens of the right place to vacation. The Russian Empress-Mother Alexandra Feodorovna came mid-century, as did the Queen of Denmark. Queen Victoria made nine visits towards the end of the century.

Americans created the summer tourist season after World War I.

The international character of the Riviera continues today in tourism, cinema, music, technology, wine and food.

Ab l'alen tir vas me l'aire
Qu'eu sen venir de Proensa!
Qu'om no sap tan dous repaire
Cum de Rozer tro c'a Vensa,
Si cum clau mars e Durensa

With my breath I draw toward me the air
That I do sense is coming from Provence
For no one knows so sweet a country
As that which spans from Rhône to Vence
Enclosed between the sea and the Durance

Peire Vidal, troubadour, twelfth century.

CHAPTER ONE

Pre-history

TERRA AMATA

The French Riviera has one of the oldest inhabited prehistoric sites in the world. Terra Amata in Nice is dated at 380,000 years ago. The inhabitants, *Homo erectus*, lived in huts on the beach and used domesticated fire. They manufactured tools out of the beach pebbles and, rarely, animal bones. They hunted elephants, rhinoceros, aurochs, deer, wild boar and rabbits. They ate seagulls, pheasants and eagles. From the sea they took turtles, eels, mussels, oysters and limpets. No human bones have been found but one human footprint has been discovered.

The nomadic inhabitants only stayed for a few days at a time at the end of spring or beginning of summer. When they arrived, they built huts with branches supported by posts. Blocks of stone delimited the oval huts, which could measure 7 to 15 metres by 4 to 6 metres. The centre of the hut was kept free of tool workings, which were confined to one area. The inhabitants sat in the centre, either on the ground or on blocks of wood. The fire was in a small ditch of 30 to 50 cm diameter, protected from wind on the north-west by a small wall.

The site compares with that in Beeches Pit in England, Menez-Dregan in Brittany, Vértesszőlős in Hungary and Zhoukoudian in China.

Terra Amata is on the western slopes of Mount Boron, 300 metres from the port of Nice. At the time of the prehistoric occupation the sea was 20 metres above its present level. Discovered in 1966, the site is a museum, which can be visited.

Other important prehistoric sites are the Grotte du Vallonnet, the Grotte du Lazaret, the Cosquer cave near Marseilles and the Vallée des Merveilles.

*

VALLONNET

Vallonnet, which is near Roquebrune-Cap-Martin, about 800 m above the bay of Menton, was discovered by a thirteen-year-old girl, Marianne Poire in 1958. She collected pieces of calcite there and called them shiny stones. The cave contains 100 tools, which have been dated to between 950,000 and 1,050,000 years old, making it one of the earliest sites of human settlement known in Europe. Large carnivores that used the cave included bears, panthers, sabre-tooth tigers and large hyenas. They brought to the cave the carcasses of herbivores, including deer, bison, small bovides, rhinoceros, horses and boars. Other species found include Eurasian jaguars, leopards, meridional elephants, early species of wolf, early foxes and cave lynxes, hippopotamus and even whales. The tools were used to break bones and eat the marrow inside. There are no signs that the humans lived in the cave. It is not open to the public.

*

LAZARET

Lazaret, which is on the west side of Mount Boron in Nice, has human remains dated at 170,000 years old. Animal carcasses have also been found, including deer, ibex, wolf, bear, lynx, birds and rodents. It is not normally open to the public but there is an annual workshop at the cave.

*

COSQUER

Not until 1985 did man find cave art on the French Riviera, which is so common in the rest of France. In that year Henri Cosquer, a diver, discovered the entrance to a cave in the Calanque de Morgiou near Marseilles, 37 m below current sea level. It contained 150 animal figures and 65 hand stencils. The contents of the Cosquer cave were not known until 1991 when three divers became lost in the cave and died. Older drawings are dated as 27,000 years old and newer drawings and animal drawings 19,000 years. The animals are bison, ibex and horses. There are also seals and what appear to be two male auks fighting over a female and jellyfish. The cave was never lived in, but remains of charcoal from fires and torches have been found.

The site cannot be visited, but one day a facsimile may be made.

*

VALLÉE DES MERVEILLES

The Vallée des Merveilles (Valley of Marvels) holds the largest quantity of open-air Bronze Age petroglyphs in Europe, after Val Camonica in Italy. It is part of the Mercantour National Park and the rock engravings are mainly to be found in two valleys, Merveilles and Fontanalba.

Most of the rocks belong to the Permo-Triassic formation, and the greater part of those on which the engravings were executed have smooth, flat or rounded surfaces, polished by the action of the glaciers in the Quaternary Ice Age. The rocks contain a little iron and the surfaces that have been exposed to the air have become weathered, and they have therefore acquired a thin patina of yellowish-red colour. The engravings have been made by repeated blows with a pointed tool of stone or metal, the punched holes being so close together that the coloured patina was removed, showing the design on the dark purplish-grey rock and against a background of the more highly coloured patinated surface. The engravings have been so long exposed to the weather that the surface has again become patinated.

The site has been quoted in travel books since the fifteenth century. In 1868, the English botanist John Traherne Moggridge was the first to date the engravings to the prehistoric period. In 1897 Clarence Bicknell, of

Bordighera, began the first major systematic study of them. At the time of his death in 1918 he had discovered, and made heel-ball rubbings of 7,428 figures in Val Fontanalba, 5,139 in the Meraviglie district, and 151 in the neighbouring valleys. The total recorded today is 27,000, spread over about 4,000 hectares. The study continues.

There are a great variety of subjects in the engravings, though figures representing horned animals far outnumber the others. Bicknell divided the engravings into eight categories: (1) horned figures, (2) ploughs, (3) weapons, (4) men, (5) huts and properties, (6) skins, (7) geometrical forms, and (8) miscellaneous indeterminable figures. The special characteristic of the Mount Bego rock figures is that they are drawn as seen from above and not in profile as in Sweden and elsewhere.

The engravers left no trace of their tools or weapons and no burial sites have been found in the district. Who they were and whence they came remains an unsolved problem. Archaeologists have dated them in the Bronze Age from 1800 to 1500 BC.

The stones can be visited from May to September depending on the accessibility and there is a museum devoted to them in Tende. Marcus Bicknell, a descendant of Clarence Bicknell, has formed the Clarence Bicknell Association to study the stones.

CHAPTER TWO

Greeks 600–390 BC

MARSEILLES

Marseilles was founded as Massalia in 600 BC. The founders were Greeks from the city of Phocaea on the Aegean coast of modern Turkey. It is known today as Foça and is 70 km north-west of Izmir, formerly Smyrna.

Before the arrival of the Greeks, the region was inhabited by the Ligures, an ancient Indo-European people with both Italic and Celtic affinities. It is possible nonetheless that the name was given by the Greeks to all the people living in the western Mediterranean area.

The Greek historian Herodotus tells us that *they were the first of the Greeks to make long voyages and it was they who opened up the region of the Adriatic, Etruria and Spain and Tartessos.* They sailed, not in merchant ships, he says, but in *pentokonters* – fifty-oared war galleys. One of the attractions of the site of Massalia was the splendid harbour, which was a good staging post en route to the Tartessos area on the Atlantic coast of the Iberian peninsular. Tartessos, which was at the mouth of the Guadalquivir, Guadalete and Tinto rivers, was an important region for trade in tin, gold, silver and copper. The site of Massalia was also attractive because the River Rhône gave access to the barbarian north, to the headwaters of the Loire and thus the Atlantic. Massalia received an important injection of colonists when, in 546 BC, Phocaea was captured by Harpagos, a general of Cyrus the Great, King of Persia and many of its inhabitants fled west.

Greek sources tell us that the founders of Massalia were led by Protis. The leader of the local Celts or Gauls, the Ligurian Segobriges tribe, Nannos, was so welcoming that he invited the Greeks to the betrothal ceremony of his daughter, Gyptis. Her father asked her to choose her husband. She rejected the Celts and chose Protis. She signalled her choice by offering him a cup of water. The proud father was so pleased, so the story goes, that he gave the Phocaeans a tract of land on which they built Massalia.

When the Carthaginians effectively took control of the southern Spanish ports and cut off the Greeks from the minerals of Tartessos, Massalia took on an important new role. It became the centre for two major trade routes through barbarian Europe, the Rhône-Saône valley and the Garonne-Gironde route to the Atlantic. The Massalians then had access to the tin of Galicia, Armorica and Cornwall. Notable among the goods flowing south to north included prestige equipment for Greek wine-drinking rituals like Rhodian flagons.

The Massalians advertised their success by building the Treasury of the Massalians at Delphi in about 530 BC.

Massalia's most famous explorer was Pytheas, who in the late fourth century BC sailed at least as far as Scotland. He wrote two books about his travels: *About the Ocean* and *Round the World*. They are no longer extant, but are widely quoted. The historians Polybius and Strabo reproduced large sections of his works, mainly in order to attack his reliability. Polybius thought Pytheas was an unprincipled rogue and a liar. Rehabilitation came only with the work of Bougainville, an eighteenth-century French mathematician and explorer.

Pytheas calculated latitudes using the gnomon, an instrument like a sundial. His calculations were extraordinarily accurate. He gave the latitude of Marseilles as 43°3′38″ north of the equator, while the true figure was 43°17′4″, an error of only about 50 km. He was the first Greek to determine that ocean tides were caused by lunar attraction.

Pytheas followed the coast north to Brittany. He landed at Belerion (Land's End) and then sailed through the Irish Sea, possibly calling at the Isle of Man. We are not certain where he went after Scotland, but perhaps to Iceland, which was called Thule in Greek, an island six days' sailing from Britain. Other possibilities are Norway, Denmark and Helgoland, the Shetland Islands and Stettin in Germany. At some point he visited Kantion, or Kent. He saw the midnight sun and 'congealed sea' (icebergs and pack ice). He went in search of the prized amber.

Another Marseilles explorer was Euthymenes, who around the same time as Pythias sailed to Dakar, Senegal and perhaps Ghana.

One of the attractions of Massalia was that from its foundation, it was a fully-fledged Greek *polis* with an army, navy, coinage and a constitution. Its stability and continuity are shown by the five names under which it has been known: Massalia (Greek), Massilia (Latin), Marisho (Provençal), Marseille (French) and Marseilles (English).

Massalia's rather louche character dates from its early days when the citizens were considered to be effeminate, wearing floor-length tunics. Moreover, 'going to Massalia' came to be used as equivalent to 'going to the dogs'.

The honeymoon with the Ligurians was not to last and when Nannos died, his son Comanus attacked the Greeks. Comanus and 7,000 of his men died.

The historian Strabo, a Roman of Greek origin, tells us that in his day Massalia was crammed with war memorials from past naval victories. These are likely to have been over the Etruscans and Carthaginians. Good relations with Rome date at least from the time of the Gallic invasion of Rome in 390 BC. Massalia and Rome then signed a treaty granting the Massaliots equal rights in Rome, as well as immunity from taxation and reserved seats in the theatre. Cicero, a great fan of Massalia, wrote of the past services to Rome, without saying exactly what they were.

However, we can assume they included the Massalian navy on which Rome could call if necessary, and a window on Gaul.

The importance of Massalia is shown by the fact that Aristotle published a treaty on its constitution, now mostly lost. We do, however, know that its governing body was a board of 600 members called the timouchoi. The laws included:

- Suicide legal, subject to official approval. Anyone who felt life was no longer worth living could make an application to the timouchoi and if successful, could be provided with a dose of hemlock at public expense.

- No pornographic theatre. It was prohibited for fear that the audience would consummate in reality what they saw counterfeited on stage.

- No unauthorised cults. The object of this prohibition was not so much religious as to get rid of beggars using it as an excuse to seek handouts, when instead they ought to be doing an honest day's work.

- Foreigners to check their weapons with the police. An officer took them at the city gates and handed them back on departure.
- Sumptuary laws imposed. Set limits for dowries and wedding dresses. Public demonstrations of mourning were forbidden, although members of the family were allowed a small private wake. Two empty coffins, one for citizens and one for slaves, were kept on permanent standby at the city gates and the deceased was conveyed to the cemetery on a farm cart.
- Restrictions on slave freedom. A freed slave could be re-enslaved if he showed himself insufficiently grateful to his former master. This could be done thrice, but then no more.
- Women not allowed wine on pain of death.

Men consumed plenty of wine. It was produced locally from the time of the founding of Massalia. But the imports from Italy were colossal. Ten million litres were eventually imported annually into Gaul from Italy, mostly through Massalia.

The Greeks brought to Provence the olive, cypress, grape, acanthus and pomegranate. The French writer André Maurois claimed the Battle of the Flowers, celebrated today in Nice and other towns of the Riviera, originated with the Greeks.

The Greeks established settlements to the east, although little is known of their dependency on Massalia.

The Roman Antonine itinerary of 150 AD lists ports along the coast. They are likely to have a Greek origin, particularly if the place-names sound Greek. These are the most important:

Cassis (Carsicis): Cassis was famous for its coral, which was regarded as superior to that produced in the Balearics, Sardinia and North Africa. There were extensive limestone quarries, and inscriptions cut on Cassis stone have been found in North Africa.

Tauroention (Greek), Tauroentum (Roman): Location unknown.

La Ciotat (Citharista): The nearby small mountain village of Ceyreste may have been the city of Citharista, a Greek foundation.

Olbia: Olbia (=Fortunate) is at L'Almanarre near the Giens peninsula between Hyères and Toulon, and is open to visitors. It is unique in France because it is the only example of a Greek and Roman town to have been preserved as a whole. It was founded as a trading post and fort around 350 BC, probably to help secure coastal traffic to and from Massalia and to protect against Ligurian expansion.

The site is square, with each side 160 m long, and is remarkable for the precision of the measurements. The blocks of houses, 11 m wide, are exactly five times the width of the streets separating them. The two main streets are 4 m and 5 m wide, intersecting at a central crossroads. The gods were not forgotten and there is a monument with the Greek inscription: "Of Aphrodite". It was probably a cross between a trading post and a fort and had a population of about a thousand.

St-Tropez (Athenopolis): The Greek settlement was probably on the site of today's Old City around the Hôtel de Ville, but no remains to confirm it have been found yet.

Antibes (Antipolis): The good Greek name means 'The City Facing'. But facing what? Scholars have discussed it for years. But no one knows. They are agreed that the Greek town was probably on the narrow strip of high ground between the present Cours Massena and the sea. The most famous artefact is the 'Antibes Stone', which is a flint worn by erosion into the shape of a roller, 64 cm long with an inscription in archaic Greek script in which Terpnon, a servant of holy Aphrodite, calls down blessings on all who set up the stone. Another claim to fame was the Antibes fish sauce and its artificial fish ponds. An inferior fish brine from Antibes called *muria* was used to treat dysentry, sciatica and coeliac disease.

Nice (Nikaia) (=Victory City): The Greek settlement was probably on the Colline du Château beside the harbour. Pliny lists it as a Massaliot foundation and Strabo adds that it was founded to secure the sea routes from the inland barbarians, i.e. Ligurians.

By the time the Greeks established Nice, the Celto-Ligurian tribe, the Vediantii, were settled in a hill-fort at Cimiez. The two settlements seem to have co-existed peacefully as the Vediantii do not figure as enemies in accounts of defence of the Massaliot communities by the Romans in 154 BC, nor on the list on the La Turbie inscription of the tribes beaten by the Romans.

Monaco (Herculis Monoeci): Monaco is a Phoenician word signifying a place for rest, a place where one stops.

It has a long history. It is first mentioned by Hecataios, the first known Greek historian, as quoted in Stephanus of Byzantium. That dates it to the sixth century BC. Later references are in Strabo and Virgil. Strabo says it was the furthest and last port reached by Massaliot coastal navigation.

*

Surprisingly neither Toulon nor Cannes appear to have had Greek settlements. Despite this, the Greeks sheltered their ships crossing between Massalia and Olbia in Toulon.

The hellenisation of Marseilles had its limits nonetheless. In the first century BC the entrance of the oppidum of the Bell (north of the city) was decorated according to a Celtic tradition, with the skulls of defeated enemies.

*

CELTS

The Celts, which the daughter Greek settlements were built to deter, had come to France from Central Europe in about 750 BC. They mostly lived in oppida, which were usually fortified encampments on defensible hilltops. Over 750 of them have been identified in the Var, Alpes-Maritimes and Gard. But they also lived in towns of some sophistication.

A Greek described them as brave, strong, individualistic to a fault, excited, talented, adaptable, living in a land rich and well-watered; a constant temptation to the conqueror.

Greek and Roman writers considered the most noteworthy activity of the Celts was head-hunting. A Greek historian says they cut off their enemies' heads and slung them on their saddlebows while they sang their victory song. They nailed them to the walls of their living rooms or embalmed them in cedar oil and kept them in chests.

Their women were famous. The historian Ammianus Marcellinus wrote: *"A Gallic woman, fighting beside her man, is match for a whole troop of foreigners. Steely-eyed, and far stronger than her husband, she swells her neck, gnashes her teeth, flexes her huge white biceps, and reins wallops and kicks as though from the twisted cords of a catapult."*

CHAPTER THREE
Romans 390 BC–313 AD

GAULS

The Romans had their first taste of the Celts, whom they called Gauls, in 390 BC when a tribe under Brennus advanced down the Tiber and defeated them at the battle of Allia. They besieged Rome for six months and only the Capitol was unconquered. They were saved by a famous warning: the honking of Juno's sacred geese.

*

PUNIC WARS

The history of the Romans in the south of France has to be seen in the context of the Punic Wars between Rome and Carthage. The first Punic War from 265 to 241 BC, which the Romans won, gave Sicily and Corsica to Rome. Excluded from the south of Italy, Carthage turned to Spain. Thus the south of France, lying between Italy and Spain, became critical.

Hannibal of Carthage launched the Second Punic War in 219 BC by attacking Rome's Spanish city, Saguntum. He entered Gaul from Spain in the spring of 218 BC with almost 100,000 men and 50 elephants, crossing the Alps into Italy. Defeated, Hannibal committed suicide in 182 BC. The Romans paid the Gauls for their help during the Second Punic War and the Massaliots contributed to the sum.

The Third Punic War from 153 to 149 BC ended with the destruction of Carthage.

*

ROMANS IN GAUL

In 189 BC a Roman governor, L. Baebius, on his way through the south of France to Spain was attacked by Ligurians and died in Marseilles. It was the first major event in the long history of the Romans in Gaul. There was thereafter almost continual trouble with the Gauls and Ligurians. In 181 BC, the Massaliots of Marseilles complained of piracy to Rome and Gaius Mattienus was sent with ten ships to deal with them.

Things eventually became so serious that Massaliot envoys went to Rome in 154 BC to appeal for help against the Ligurians, who were now threatening the Greek cities of Nice and Antibes. A commission of enquiry determined that the culprits were the Oxybii and Deciatae tribes who lived south and west of the River Var. The Romans sent Quintus Opimius to suppress them, which he did decisively in two battles. The Massaliots took over their territories and some of the smaller tribes had to submit hostages. A further punishment was that transalpine people were banned from growing olives and vines. The Romans stayed throughout the winter, but still did not see the need to establish a permanent presence in the area. Cicero underlined the importance of the relationship with Marseilles when he commented that Rome could never have triumphed over the transalpine Gauls without the help of the Massaliots.

*

One of the reasons the Romans responded so readily to the appeals for help was trade. Southern Gaul was an important market for Italian wine and oil. By the first century BC the annual import of wine into Gaul has been estimated at 100,000 hectolitres. Also important was the export from Gaul to Italy of slaves. More than 100,000 new slaves were required in Italy every year. It has been estimated that in non-war years, 15,000 came from Gaul.

The historian Diodorus Siculus described the Gallic relationship between wine and slaves:

> *They are exceedingly fond of wine and sate themselves with the unmixed wine imported by merchants; their desire makes them drink*

it greedily and when they become drunk they fall into a stupor or into a maniacal disposition. And therefore many Italian merchants with their usual love of cash look on the Gallic craving for wine as their treasure. They transport the wine by boat on the navigable rivers and by wagon through the plains and receive in return for it an incredibly high price. For one amphora of wine they get in return a slave – a servant in return for a drink.

(The average size of an amphora was 20 to 25 litres or 4½ to 5½ gallons.)

The Greek historian Posidonius, who visited southern Gaul, described a Celtic feast where the wine must have played an important role:

The Celts sometimes engage in single combat at dinner. Assembling in arms they engage in a mock battle of mutual thrust-and-parry, but sometimes wounds are inflicted and the irritation caused by this may even lead to the slaying of the opponent unless the bystanders hold them back. And in former times, when the hindquarters were served up, the bravest hero took the thigh piece, and if another man claimed it they stood up and fought in single combat to death.

In 125 BC the Massaliots called again for help from Rome. They were being threatened by the Saluvii; a tribe living to the north of Marseilles. Rome sent two legions under the command of the consul M. Fulvius Flaccus, who won battles against the Saluvii, but also against the Vocontii from farther north and the Ligurians. In 124 BC, Rome sent another consular army under C. Sextius Calvinus, who in 122 BC founded a castellum, which he named Aquae Sextiae (Aix-en-Provence). That marked the clear defeat of the Gauls and the definitive presence of Rome. After they had defeated Spain, Rome wanted to secure the passage from the Alps to the Pyrenees. Sextius cleared the coast of Gaul and put a strip of 1,400 to 2,200 metres under the Massaliots. The Provincia Transalpina, which was to become Gallia Narbonensis (Narbonese Gaul), was established in 121 BC. It stretched from the Mediterranean to Lake Geneva. The border between Transalpina and Italy was the River Var. The consul Ahenobarbus Domitius created a western highway into Spain, the Via Domitia. The citizen colony of Narbo Martius (Narbonne) was founded in 118 BC. Gaul, beyond the Province of Transalpina, was called Gallia Comata – 'Long-haired Gaul'.

The Roman measures against the Celts were inadequate and Rome suffered in the Cimbric Wars when a horde of Celts and Germans rampaged throughout much of Europe. In 113 BC they defeated a Roman army on the Danube. They crossed the Rhine in 109 BC and stormed through Gaul for a decade, inflicting a series of defeats on the Romans. Not until 101 BC did the Romans defeat the barbarians, although there was periodic trouble in the following three decades until Pompey arrived and set up the legal framework for Transalpina of the *Lex Provinciae.*

*

LIFE UNDER THE ROMANS

The trial in 69 BC on a charge of malfeasance in the office of the Roman governor of the Provincia Narbonenis, M. Fonteius, who ruled from 76 to 74 BC, shows us what life could be like on the Riviera under the Romans. Cicero defended him from the Gaulish plaintiffs, who were clad in plaid and trousers, which to Romans always symbolised barbarism. The plaintiffs claimed Fonteius had drafted cavalry from them, quartered soldiers on them, requisitioned grain, made them work on road repairs and taxed their wine. They said he got kickbacks from the tax collectors; for a fee he exempted individuals from road work; he turned a blind eye to fraudulent contractors and illegally confiscated property. One of the most extraordinary arguments Cicero advanced in his favour was that he should not be found guilty because his sister was a Vestal Virgin. Cicero got him acquitted. Two years later, Fonteius bought an expensive house in Naples. The Emperor Tiberius remarked of tax policy: *"We should shear our sheep, not skin them."*

Only when Julius Caesar arrived in 58 BC was there a major offensive against the Gauls. But the Gauls Caesar was fighting from 58–51 BC were not the Gauls of what is now the Riviera, who were already in the Roman province of Transalpina, but the Gauls to the north, whose conquest he described in his famous history of the Gallic Wars. In Transalpina, Caesar had promoted some of the indigenous leaders, therefore he did not have to fight in the region when he was fighting the Gallic Wars. Caesar slaughtered up to a million people. Not that the Gauls were exactly peace-loving; one Greek visitor in the early first century BC had been shocked to find enemy heads pinned up at the entrance to Gallic houses. But, he conceded, you eventually got used to the sight.

*

POMPEY, CAESAR AND ANTONY

Marseilles played an important role in the civil war between Pompey and Caesar when it broke out in January 49 BC. It chose the wrong side in supporting Pompey. Caesar had visited Marseilles around April 49 BC and had appealed to leading citizens to support him. They initially took a middle path and, true to their conservative and legalistic policy, came down on the side of Pompey when the fleet of Pompey's ally Domitius arrived. Caesar's troops under Trebonius besieged Marseilles for six months and it fell towards the end of the year.

Caesar treated Marseilles with some moderation, but the Gaulish territory previously controlled by Marseilles was reduced to a very small area round it, and the city lost all its vessels. He left two legions there, but did not formally take it over. It maintained its status as a *civitas foederata*, a city controlled by alliance or treaty. Nice remained subject to it, as did Carsicis (Cassis) and the Stoechades Insulae (Iles d'Hyères).

Antibes was detached from Marseilles and became an *Italiote* city, which meant a Greek city in Italy. The importance of Antibes is shown by the fact that it was fed by no less than two aqueducts. One drew water from the Ruisseau Bouillide some 7 km to the west-north-west and the other from the River Brague near Biot, about 5 km to the north-north-west. Of the Iles de Lérins, Lero (Ile Ste-Marguerite) was more important in Roman times than Lerina (Ile St-Honorat). The Roman historian Pliny reports the existence of a town on Lero called Berconum.

The assassination of Julius Caesar in 44 BC was followed by Mark Antony taking over Gaul in May 43 BC. In November Mark Antony, Aemilius Lepidus and Octavian (later called Augustus) united in the second triumvirate. Mark Antony was given command of Cisalpine and transalpine Gaul, and Lepidus Gallia Narbonensis and Spain. Cisalpine Gaul, which lay to the east of Nice, became part of Italy in 42 BC. By 41 BC, Mark Antony governed all of the east and the Gallic provinces through his legates.

*

OCTAVIAN BECOMES AUGUSTUS

The writs changed again in 40 BC when Mark Antony relinquished Gaul but retained the east. Octavian took over the west. In 36 BC Lepidus was forced into semi-retirement.

When Octavian became sole ruler in 29 BC, he visited southern Gaul and thereafter paid it great attention. One of his first acts was to make the town of Forum Julii (Fréjus), which had been founded by Julius Caesar in 49 BC, his naval base. It later became a veteran colony for soldiers. It was famous as the birthplace in 40 AD of Cn. Julius Agricola, governor of Britain. It had many of the structures of an important Roman town, including an amphitheatre and a theatre.

The Romans built 300 aqueducts in Gaul. The aqueduct serving Fréjus was one of the finest and much of it still stands today. It brought water into the town from the River Siagnole some 30 km to the north, and was probably built in the second century AD.

Most renowned of the other towns today is Athenopolis (St-Tropez), which was under Massalian control.

In January 27 BC, the Senate bestowed on Octavian the title Augustus. In his second visit to Provence in that year he reorganised Southern Gaul as the province of Gallia Narbonensis. He left Agrippa in charge. Probably in 22 BC Augustus handed back transalpine Gaul to the

Senate, under whose authority it had previously lain. In 14 BC Augustus took the area north of Nice on both sides of the River Var and constituted it as the province of Alpes Maritimae. It was later broken up into three smaller provinces. The original capital was Cemenelum (Cimiez) to the north of Nice. Other important Roman towns were Vintium (Vence), Salinae (Castellane), Eturamina (Thorame), Brigomagus (Briançonnet) and Glanate (Glandèves). Antipolis (Antibes) had Latin rights, which gave some senior inhabitants Roman citizenship.

The Alpine Trophy at La Turbie, above Monaco, on the highest point of Via Julia Augusta is a tribute to Emperor Augustus and was built in 7–6 BC to commemorate his suppression from 24–14 BC of forty-five tribes of Alpine people. We have to wonder why Julius Caesar had not conquered them half a century before. The Roman historian Appian said that it was a wonder to him that so many great Roman armies traversing the Alps to conquer the Gauls and Spaniards should have overlooked these tribes. Even Caesar, he said, did not achieve their subjection during the ten years he was fighting the Gauls and wintering in that very country. Appian's opinion was that Caesar seemed to have delayed putting an end to the troubles with these tribes because of the Gallic War and the strife with Pompey.

The monument was pillaged over the centuries, but the ruins were classified as a historical monument in 1865. An American financed its restoration in 1934. He was Edward Tuck, a wealthy financier. He also had the distinction of financing the first graduate business school in the United States, the Amos Tuck School of Business Administration at Dartmouth College. The monument can be visited.

Henceforth the Midi enjoyed three centuries of peace and prosperity: the *Pax Romana*. Its economy was based on the production of grain, olive oil, wine, pigs and sheep. An indicator of prosperity was the large number of monuments and structures of this period.

The edict of Carcalla in 212 provided that all free men of the empire became citizens. The motivation was that all would be eligible for service in the legions and pay inheritance tax. A consequence was that Marseilles became part of Narbonensis. The connection of Nice with Marseilles ended and Nice was attached to the Alpes-Maritimes with its capital in Cimiez.

Diocletian, who reigned as emperor from 284 to 305, made further structural changes in 284. Narbonensis was divided into two: Narbonensis to the west of the Rhône and Viennoise to the east. The Alpes-Maritimes added the territories of Digne, Senez and Embrun. Embrun replaced Cimiez as the capital of the province.

The local aristocracy included some Celts, who had risen through the civil service and had married into the Roman local elite. The most favoured of these local aristocrats became knights or even senators.

The Gauls who had risen in the hierarchy did not always treat their fellow countrymen well. Julius Licinus, a freed Gallic slave, who collected taxes, used a change in the calendar to trick some citizens into paying more taxes than were due. They complained to Augustus when he visited the province in 16 BC, but it seems the wily Julius got away unpunished.

Gauls were an important part of the Roman army. The British and Rhine legions were increasingly recruited from Narbonensis. So perhaps it is not too far-fetched a conceit to see the flow from south to north reversed two millennia later as the Germans and British headed for the Riviera.

The success of Augustus in Gallia Narbonensis was struck by tragedy. He had adopted as his son Julius Caesar Lucius, his grandson; a possible future emperor, whose mother was his daughter Julia. In 2 AD the nineteen-year-old left Rome for his first provincial command in Spain. He stopped in Massalia, fell ill and died. Augustus was devastated.

CHAPTER FOUR

Christians and Barbarians
313–855

CHRISTIANS

The Edict of Milan in 313 decreed that Christians had complete religious freedom.

Christianity came relatively early to the Riviera. Churches were built in Marseilles (314), Nice (314), Fréjus (374), Antibes (398), Vence (419), Cimiez (439) and Toulon (441). Monasteries were founded at Lérins (Cannes)(410) and St-Victor (Marseilles) (416). (Dates are approximate.) St-Victor, a complex of monasteries for both men and women, was founded by John Cassian, a monk from the east, and served as a model for later monastic development elsewhere in Europe. The monks of the Riviera, in Lérins and St-Victor were important for their missionary fervour. The Iles de Lérins have a long and distinguished history. Excavations have uncovered houses, paintings, mosaics and ceramics from around the third century BC to the first century AD. When Honoratus of Arles founded a monastery on the larger of the two islands, women were banned. His sister Marguerite therefore set up a convent on the other island where Honoratus could come to see her regularly.

The Council of Arles in 314 included representatives from Marseilles and Nice.

The Riviera was not without religious ascetics. In the 570s, Hospicius lived in a tower outside Nice wrapped in a hair shirt and chains. He was reputed to perform miracles.

*

BARBARIANS

Visigoths, Ostrogoths, Vandals, Huns, Franks, Burgundians, Saxons and Lombards invaded Provence at various times after the collapse of the Roman Empire in the fifth century. The Franks had already invaded Gaul from the north in 341, but did not take over Provence until 536. Around 381 the Romans divided the province of Narbonne into three: the Alpes-Maritimes, Narbonne II, including part of the west of what is now the Riviera and specifically Fréjus and Antibes, and Viennoise, including Marseilles and the Stoechades islands (now the Iles d'Hyères) and the contiguous coast. Archaeological digs have shown us that the region prospered, particularly in agriculture. The main crop was cereals, with viniculture becoming increasingly important.

In 400 the Roman Emperor Honorius had declared Arles the capital of the Three Gauls – France, Britain and Spain.

In 410 the Visigoths, whom the Romans regarded as barbarians from the east, sacked Rome. Provence saw the repercussions when in 413 the Visigoth King Alaric passed through the territory en route to Spain. The Visigoths set up a kingdom in Aquitaine in 413–414 and took possession of its capital, Palladia Tolosa, the modern Toulouse, in 418, but initially failed to take Marseilles. That conquest came later. The Visigoth King Theodoric I allied with the Roman military ruler, Aetius, and defeated the Huns, led by Attila, after they had invaded Gaul in 451 at the Catalaunian Plains, where Theodoric perished. It is thought to have been near today's Châlons-en-Champagne in the department of the Marne. The death toll on both sides was enormous. Many historians believe that the battle was decisive in human history. It was the first major battle since the death of Constantine I where a predominantly Christian force faced a predominantly pagan opponent. The Christians won.

The impact of the invaders was colossal. Literacy levels fell, building in stone almost ceased, the amount of smelting work fell to that of prehistoric times and long-distance trade collapsed.

There was rarely a clear-cut division between the immigrants and Romans. A significant number of barbarians were part of the Roman army before the invasions. Most of the immigrants were prepared to work within a framework that accepted the existence of the Roman Empire. They often had a treaty or *foedus* that involved the settlement of the people under their king in return for military service.

Roman Gaul had many similarities to British India, where the British ruled and where Indians, many of whom had descended from the north earlier, provided soldiers. Intermarriage existed between conqueror and conquered, and religious worship was free.

In 474 Julius Nepos became emperor and in 475, he made an agreement with the Visigothic King Euric that allowed the imperial government to recover the territories in Provence occupied by Euric earlier. In 476, in the name of the empire, Euric conquered Marseilles and control of much of Provence fell back into the hands of the Visigoths. Julius Nepos had been overthrown in 475 and had been succeeded by Romulus Augustulus. The year 476 saw the end of the Western Roman Empire, with the overthrow of Romulus Augustulus by the Germanic general Odoacer.

*

OSTROGOTHS, BURGUNDIANS AND FRANKS

New players appeared on the scene in 489 when the Ostrogoths led by another Theodoric invaded Italy. The Huns had driven the Ostrogoths from the Ukraine to Hungary but they sought a more permanent home and eventually found it in Italy, where Theodoric took the title of king. He personally murdered his predecessor Odoacer at a banquet, to which he had invited him. Odoacer's wife was imprisoned and left to starve to death. Odoacer's supporters and their families were massacred. But most of Theodoric's reign of thirty-three years was blameless and Italy and eastern Provence benefited from the rule of one of the great monarchs of his time.

The Franks and Burgundians tried unsuccessfully to exploit the decline of Visigoth rule in Provence in 507–8.

However, in 507, in alliance with the Burgundians, the Frankish King Clovis, who had become king of the Franks in 481, defeated and killed Euric's son Alaric II at the Battle of Vouillé. Clovis converted to Christianity, probably in 496 or 508.

Theodoric seized Marseilles and annexed much of Provence in 508 in order to secure the western approaches to Italy. After Vouillé, the Franks and Burgundians headed to Provence, to conquer Arles, which was until then ruled by the Visigoths who were controlling the commercial traffic between northern Europe and the Mediterranean. Therefore, the Ostrogoths, led by Theodoric, upset by the threat to their own kingdom, decided to interfere. He first tried after Vouillé to reconcile the enemies and it was only in June 508 that he liberated the city of Arles. With Franks and Burgundians contained under the tutelage of the Ostrogoths, Provence benefited from a period of tranquillity, sometimes called *Pax ostrogothica*, until the middle of the 530s. Arles underwent a revival both political and ecclesiastical with the restoration of the prefecture of the praetorium and the status of primacy.

The Franks often got a bad press from near-contemporary historians. Fredegar implicitly compared the sons of Clovis to bears and wolves and his grandsons to dogs.

Francia – the kingdom of the Franks – was divided up among the four sons of Clovis on his death in 511, although there was only a single *regnum francorum*. They were Clothar, Childebert, Theuderic and Chlodomer. Clothar took Soissons and ruled in the old Salic heartlands, but also including Orange and Gap; Theuderic took Rheims and north-eastern Gaul; Childebert was to rule Paris and north-western Gaul and Chlodomer Orléans and central Gaul.

In 523, Childebert and his brothers fought a war against Burgundy in which Chlodomer died. Concerned that the three sons of Chlodomer would inherit the kingdom of Orléans, Clothar conspired with Childebert to oust them. They sent a representative to their mother Clotilde, who as the queen mother had authority as the head of the family line. The representative presented a pair of scissors and a sword, offering her the choice to shear the three young boys, thereby depriving them of the long hair considered a symbol of royal power, or to have them killed. She famously replied, *"It is better for me to see them dead rather than shorn, if they are not raised to the kingship."* After the murder of Chlodomer's two eldest children – the third escaping to a monastic life – Childebert annexed the cities of Chartres and Orléans. During the sixth century the only non-Germanic name a Merovingian king gave to his son was Samson.

In 534, after much warfare, the Burgundian kingdom had become subject to the Franks, although the Burgundians were allowed to keep their own law.

Theuderic died in 534. His son was Theudebert, who died in 548.

In 536 Vitigis, a later Ostrogoth successor to Theodoric, ceded the Ostrogoth territory in Provence to the Franks, along with 2,000 pounds of gold, marking the end of the Ostrogoth domination. The purpose of the transfer for the Ostrogoths was to get Frankish military support for Vitigis in Italy. Childebert's brothers guaranteed Arles and Marseilles would go to him. For the first time the area of France roughly similar to what we know as the coastal Riviera was governed as a discrete unit by a single ruler. Childebert ruled from the Mediterranean coast south-west of Arles to just east of Nice from 536 to 558.

There was another Frankish carve-up in 561 on the death of Clothar when his four sons, Charibert, Guntram, Chilperic and Sigibert I shared the spoils. Charibert got the ancient kingdom of Childebert I, plus Aquitaine and Provence; Guntram got Burgundy and part of the kingdom of Orléans; Chilperic was given the territories north of the kingdom of Soissons and Sigibert the kingdom of Metz. The rule of Provence varied according to the perennial wars between the Frankish rulers.

The Franks were keen get their hands on taxes in Provence, which they pursued assiduously. One of the best-known officials who ensured the efficient collection of taxes was Parthenius, a Gallo-Roman and grandson of the emperor Avitus. He was governor of Provence. The Franks used many aristocrats of Roman descent as administrators and bishops. In a later post, Parthenius so infuriated the mob by his tax collecting that they pursued him into a church in Trier and stoned him to death. Gregory of Tours, the historian, wrote that he broke wind in public without any consideration for those present, but that was not the reason for his stoning.

After the death of Theodoric in 526, Provence eventually benefited from another great ruler when Justinian became emperor in Constantinople in 527. He was the first emperor since 476 who determined to recover the lost provinces of the Roman west. By 562 he had regained all of Italy, and also much of Provence. Another of his achievements was to reform the whole corpus of Roman law.

But in 568 Italy was invaded from today's Hungary by the Lombards, under their great King Alboin. They soon crossed into south-eastern Gaul and attacked the territories of the Frankish King Guntram. They effectively closed the Mediterranean to the Franks. Initially they had great success, killed many and acquired great booty. But the second raid, which got as far as Embrun, was a disaster. A Gallo-Roman general, Eunius Mummolus, fighting for Guntram, defeated them and a group of accompanying Saxons. The last major attack was in 574 when three Lombard dukes attacked southern Gaul and devastated territories as far west as the Rhône before they were driven out by Mummolus.

Guntram was considered to be a 'good' king. In 588 when the people of Marseilles were suffering from a severe swelling in the groin – bubonic plague – he ordered the entire people to assemble in church, eat and drink nothing but barley bread and pure water and keep the vigils. The historian does not tell us if they were cured or not. King Guntram could also perform miracles.

The career of Siagrius, patricius of Provence, the equivalent of a duke, gives a fascinating insight into the Franks of the early seventh century. He was the son of Salvius and Herchenfreda, both members of the Gallo-Roman aristocracy from Albi in the south of France. Chlothar II was a descendant of Clovis, who had become king of Neustria, which was the western part of the kingdom of the Franks, in 584 and Burgundy and Austrasia, which was the north-eastern part, from 613 to 638. His son was Dagobert I, who was king of Austrasia in 623 and Neustria and Austrasia from 629 to 638. The two monarchs ran a finishing school in their court for the aristocracy in order to groom them for office. To that school went Siagrius, later returning to Albi as count of the city before his Provençal appointment.

The cosmopolitan nature of Francia is shown by the fact that other pupils of the school, whom Siagrius may well have met, were Uscfrea, son of King Edwin of Northumbria in England and Edwin's second wife Æthelburg of Kent, and Yffi, grandson of Edwin by his first wife, Cwenburh. Æthelburg, who was half Merovingian, sent the offspring into the safe-keeping of her cousin Dagobert I after Edwin was killed in battle in 632 or 633.

However, Æthelburg may well have had doubts about the wisdom of sending the boys to Dagobert's court if she had heard the rumours of dissipation that caused the mother of Siagrius to write to his brother, counselling him above all to preserve his chastity. On the other hand, she would not have needed to worry for long because the Venerable Bede tells us they died in infancy.

The Franks began to come into their own. The founder of the dynasty was Merovech, supposedly born of a sea monster. As we have seen, Clovis had become king of the Franks in the Merovingian dynasty in 481. Five years later he had defeated the Roman army at Soissons and had started to extend his kingdom.

The reader will not be alone in puzzling at the difference between Franks, Merovingians and Carolingians. The Franks were a people who originated in Germany and invaded northern France. The Merovingians were a Frankish dynasty under their King Clovis, who ruled from 481/2 to 511. The Carolingians were a Frankish dynasty founded by Pippin III who overthrew Childeric III, the last of the Merovingian rulers, in 750 and the dynasty was named after Pippin's son Charlemagne, king from 768 and emperor from 800.

Franks were found in high office in the Roman imperial service. They were masters of cavalry, even consuls. The Franks borrowed many Roman forms of government and the Roman form and the Latin language of documents. Latin was the royal language and was one of the principal influences making for social homogeneity in early medieval France. The Merovingians considered themselves within Roman imperial authority. The imperial approbation was a source of strength and prestige.

*

CAROLINGIANS

As the seventh century advanced, Provence became semi-independent. Only when Charles Martel, 'the Hammer', probably an illegitimate descendant of the Merovingians, defeated all comers from 715 to 719 and took the title of 'mayor of the palace' of the Merovingian kingdom, was rule largely centralised.

The relationship between the mayor of the palace and the king was akin to the eventual relationship between the shogun and emperor in Japan, or – to push the analogy a bit – between a prime minister and a king or queen in a European constitutional monarchy. But for the last five years of his life, Charles was able to rule without a king.

There is a myth that Charles Martel defeated the Arabs in a famous victory near Poitiers in 732 or 733. In fact he was fighting against a range of enemies of the Frankish kingdom. Among them were the Saracens, which meant at the time anyone but the Christians – even the Basques. These Saracens were not all Arabs, but mostly Gascons, Basques and Spaniards converted to Islam. The Arabs (and especially converted peoples from North Africa) conquered the Visigothic kingdom in 711.

Furthermore Charles Martel was not alone in that battle. It was an army of knights of the Frankish kingdoms and duchies of Aquitaine and Vasconia, led by Charles Martel, and Eudes, Duke of Vasconia and Aquitaine.

But if historians still debate the importance of the battle of Poitiers in stopping the Arab raids, they all agree that it was decisive in the establishment of the Carolingian dynasty.

Charles still had to suppress in Provence the patricius Antener and then the *dux* Maurontus, whom he fought in the 730s when the rebels were sometimes allied with the Saracens. Maurontus had to flee for refuge to the Alps.

The revolt was a resistance of the Roman population against Frankish lordship. The subjugation by the Franks was long and hard for most of the 730s and left the area devastated for over a generation. Charles' first attack on Marseilles was only temporarily successful. In 738 he had to make another expedition with the support of the Lombard King Liutprand. By

739 he had achieved complete suppression of Provence and the expulsion of the Saracens. That year marked the definitive absorption of the region into the Frankish kingdom.

The rebels were locally assertive. Antener confiscated the estates of the monastery of St-Victor and made the abbot place on the high altar all the records of landholdings. They were then burnt to stop any subsequent abbots from claiming the property.

By his death in 741, much of Provence came under Charles Martel's son, Pippin III. In 743 the Carolingians found it useful to raise another Merovingian, Childeric III, to the throne. But in 751 Pippin deposed him, with the endorsement of the Pope.

When Charles Martel's grandson Charlemagne conquered Lombardy in 773–4 and controlled Aquitaine, Bavaria and Saxony, Provence, which had become part of Charlemagne's kingdom in 771, was part of a vast tract of Europe of 600 counties and 180 dioceses. Provence was administered by counts and bishops and inspected by Charlemagne's *missi*, a team of high officials, one a cleric and one a layman. In 800 the Pope crowned Charlemagne Emperor of the Romans. He died in 814 and was succeeded by his son Louis I, who died in 840. For arcane reasons Louis was known in Germany as 'the Pious' and in France as 'the Debonaire'.

The first half of the ninth century again saw attacks on Provence by the Saracens. In 813 they ravaged Nice and in 838 attacked Marseilles, destroyed the Benedictine abbey of St-Victor and took many captives. The church was reorganised by the Carolingians, but the trade and the ports were in decline and there was a lack of settlers.

From 835 a succession of dukes dominated Provence. In 845 Fulcrad rebelled and the Emperor Lothar I, grandson of Charlemagne, had himself to come to Provence to treat with him. He appointed Gérard, Count of Vienne as governor. Lothar had acquired Provence following the Treaty of Verdun of 843 between him and his brothers. The treaty divided Charlemagne's empire into three: West Francia, which would become the kingdom of France (Charles the Bald); East Francia, which eventually became Germany (Louis the German); and the Middle Kingdom, which became known as Lotharingia (Lothar). However, only subsequent historical convention sees these partitions as creating distinct nation states. Lotharingia later had three sections: from the North Sea to Metz; an extended Burgundia, including Provence; and northern Italy. Burgundia also in due course became divided in three: the Duchy of Burgundy in the north-west; the Kingdom of Upper Burgundy in the north; and the Kingdom of Lower Burgundy, synonymous with Provence, in the south.

CHAPTER FIVE

Kingdoms of Provence 855–1246

KINGS AND EMPERORS

The first king of Provence was created when, before his death in 855, Lothar invested his son Charles as king. But on the death of Charles of Provence in 863 his brother Louis II, king of Italy and emperor, who took over Provence, was so preoccupied in Italy that Provence again became quasi-independent under its counts, bishops and landed proprietors. When Louis died in 875 Charles the Bald took over Italy and most of Provence, including the Riviera, and was crowned emperor. He appointed his brother-in-law Boso to the duchy of Provence. Charles the Bald died in 877 and Boso was elected by leading laypersons and bishops as king of Provence (also known as Lower Burgundy) in 879. After his death, his son Louis was crowned king of Provence in 887 and was crowned emperor in 901. But he upset the magnate Berengar of Friuli in northern Italy to whom he had broken a promise, who captured and blinded him in 905. Thereafter he was known as Louis the Blind and he retired to Provence, which he theoretically ruled until his death in 928. But his incapacity meant he confided the practical rule to his cousin Hugh of Arles. He made him Duke of Provence.

Two grandsons of Charles the Bald had noteworthy deaths. Louis III died in 882 of injuries incurred while chasing a young woman on a horse for a joke while she fled into her father's house. Two years later his brother Carloman died in a hunting accident.

Provence had reverted to King Rudolf II of Burgundy on the death of Louis, but Hugh of Arles, who was king of Italy from 928 to 933, was in control through some complex kingdom-swapping arrangements until his death in 947. The deal involved Rudolf becoming king of a joint kingdom of Upper and Lower Burgundy.

Europe was cosmopolitan, showing little regard for distance, as a Provençal marriage shows. Constance of Provence married Robert II of France; they produced Henry I, who in 1051 married Anna of Kiev, daughter of Yaroslav I, Archduke of Kiev. The French kings had been having difficulties in finding brides of monarchical status to whom they were not already related so they turned to distant Russia for a solution. Contemporary chroniclers conveniently called Yaroslav a king.

(Some centuries later Louis XIV failed to be as aware of Russian personalities as his predecessors. In 1657 he addressed a letter to Tsar Michael unaware that he had been dead for twelve years.)

Provence was prosperous at this time, with much commerce in its many ancient cities. Castles started to be built, notably on the Riviera in Cagnes, Grasse, Mougins and Nice. The Christian Church gave it continuity and stability. Abbeys were built in Vence and St-Pons. Local magnates often controlled the bishoprics, as in Marseilles, Nice, Antibes and Grasse. The monastery of Montmajour in Provence was important in carrying out reform in local monasteries.

*

SARACENS

The running sore was the Saracens. The Saracens were not driven out of the south of France until 973. In the meantime they had destroyed Fréjus. They had set up pirate nests, such as Fraxinetum, now La Garde-Freinet, Tourrettes-Levens and Eze on the Riviera to launch their attacks on the pilgrim and merchant traffic crossing the Alps. The hero who defeated them was William I, who had become margrave of Provence in 968 and was known as 'the Liberator'. He was the son of Boso II of Arles.

In July 972 the Saracens kidnapped the abbot of Cluny, a Provençal, and demanded the enormous ransom of 1,000 silver livres. William mounted an expedition lasting several months and rescued him. The gratitude of the inhabitants of Provence was unbounded.

With the aid of the counts of the High Alps and the viscounts of

Marseilles and Fos, William finally routed the Saracens at the Battle of Tourtour in 973. His reward from King Conrad of Burgundy was the region east of the Rhône. Provence now became an independent principality governed by its military aristocracy. Some historians believe the departure of the Saracens marked a new era of prosperity with towns coming back into their own, with new institutions, such as the consulates, and judicial systems based on Roman law. Others believe it came later under the influence of the Church. Society was not markedly feudal. Abbeys greatly benefited from the prosperity. The Church sought to separate itself from the secular power.

The Riviera had to bear the burden of piracy even after the Saracens had been expelled in 973. Known as Barbary pirates, they mostly came from North Africa and seized inhabitants as slaves and also ransomed them. In 1154 Pope Hadrian IV, the Englishman Nicholas Breakspear, asked the consuls and inhabitants of Grasse to protect the monks of Lérins from the pirates. In 1243 the Pope moved the bishopric from Antibes to Grasse because of the piracy.

Charles II in 1302 set up thirty-two beacons from the mouth of the Rhône to La Turbie to warn of the approach of pirates.

When Nice came under Savoy, the pirates came from Nice and Monaco and attacked Antibes, Cannes and La Napoule.

Even as late as 1814, the Allies promised Napoleon they would protect the island of Elba to which he was exiled from Barbary pirates.

William I abdicated, became a monk and died in 993 or 994. He was succeeded as margrave by his elder brother Rotbild II, and as count by his son William II.

The kingdom of Provence became part of what came to be known as the Holy Roman Empire in 1032 on the death of Rudolf III, king of the Second Kingdom of Burgundy – also known as the Kingdom of Arles because of its capital.

It was bequeathed as part of Burgundy to the German king and emperor Conrad II, known as Conrad Pacifus. He was aptly named, particularly given the great troubles in northern France. Conrad II was famed for being late for his coronation because on the way he had stopped to hear pleas from a serf, a widow and an orphan.

Provence, now a margravate of the Holy Roman Empire in the imperial Kingdom of Burgundy, became known as the county of Provence. A crucial change occurred in 1081 when Bernard II, count and margrave of Provence, renounced allegiance to the empire and swore fealty to the papacy. This symbolically cut the remaining ties with the old kingdom of Burgundy and eventually enabled the transfer of the whole of Provence to the French crown without challenge from Germany.

*

BARCELONA RULE

Complicated marriages caused Provence to come under Toulouse, but in 1112 the rule of much of Provence passed to Barcelona. The reason for this extraordinary development was that in 1112 Ramon Berenguer III, who was Count of Barcelona jointly with his uncle Berenguer Ramon II from 1086 and solely from 1097, married Douce of Provence, heiress to the margravate of Provence through her mother. Ramon Berenguer III in Barcelona and I in Provence, was descended from Roger, the old Count of Carcassonne, who died in 1002. There was a war between Count Alfonse-Jordan of Toulouse (so named because he was born on a crusade and baptised in the river Jordan), who ruled from 1119 to 1148, and Ramon Berenguer I, Count of Barcelona and Provence, which Ramon Berenguer won. The war ended in a peace treaty in 1125 that divided the area. Barcelona got the coastal lands between the Rhône, the Durance, the Alps and the sea, called the county of Provence. Toulouse got the much smaller area north of the Durance, called the marquisate. They jointly held some towns, including Avignon.

Toward the end of his reign, Ramon Berenguer I became a Templar and in 1131 gave Provence to his younger son, Berenguer Ramon. The inversion of the names presumably carried some deep meaning, such as that of the younger son, and was not meant solely to confuse. Ramon Berenguer I died in 1131 and his son Berenguer Ramon died in 1144. Ramon Berenguer II, his brother, succeeded until 1162.

Raymond de Baux, an ally of Alfonse-Jordan, and the counts of Provence fought from 1143 in what were known as the Baussenque Wars, which were settled in a treaty in 1156.

In 1166 Berenguer Ramon III, who had succeeded his uncle, died in the plain of the River Loup from an arrow shot in a military expedition against Nice, which at the instigation of the Genoese, staged a rebellion against Barcelona. He had promised his daughter Douce in marriage to Raymond V of Toulouse, but on the death of Berenguer Ramon III, Raymond V pulled a clever trick by marrying his widow, Richeza of Poland, to secure his hold over Douce.

Ramon Berenguer III was succeeded by his four-year-old cousin Alphonse I the Chaste, King of Aragon and Count of Barcelona from 1162 to 1196 and Count of Provence from 1166 to 1168. He was succeeded by his brother, Ramon Berenguer IV as Count of Provence from 1168 to 1181, followed by his brother Sanche as Count of Provence until 1185. Alphonse II, son of Alphonse the Chaste was Count of Provence until 1209.

In this period a number of towns were semi-independent. Grasse, for example, was ruled by consuls who were elected annually, and called itself a republic. In 1179 Grasse made a treaty with Pisa. However, when Genoa and Pisa fell out in 1198 it switched sides and allied with Genoa until 1420. Grasse was important and supplied France, Italy and Spain with its famous leather, soap and oils. Other towns that made treaties included Hyères, Toulon and Marseilles.

In 1191 the Genoese took possession of Monaco and in 1297, the long reign of the Grimaldi family began. The Grimaldis allied themselves with France, except from 1524 to 1641, when they were under the protection of Spain. The Grimaldis later bought Roquebrune and Menton but sold them to France in 1861.

Alfonse-Jordan's son, Raymond V of Toulouse, stirred up trouble with Alphonse I in the mid-twelfth century, but was defeated in 1176 and forced to accept the 1125 settlement in the Treaty of Jarnègues. Raymond V renounced on behalf of himself and his step-daughter Douce all claims on Barcelonan Provence.

Alphonse I created in Provence the first elements of centralised power with a chancellery and professional and permanent judges.

Squabbling between Barcelona and Toulouse continued to near the end of the century, but Barcelona came out on top. Turmoil followed the death of Alphonse II in 1213. Genoa took over Nice and the county of Provence was divided between the supporters of Gersende de Forcalquier, widow of Alphonse II, and Nuno, cousin of Alphonse II. In 1216 a group of Provençal citizens rescued Ramon Berenguer V, son of Alphonse II, from Aragonese captivity, thus marking the end of Barcelonan rule of Provence.

Ramon Berenguer V was unusual in that he spent his whole reign in Provence. He achieved much, including ending the independence of a number of towns, including Grasse in 1227 and, after a military expedition, Nice in 1229. With the exception of Marseilles, which in 1230 gave itself to Toulouse to preserve its independence, all Provence eventually recognised the Count's authority. Other achievements included alliance with the King of France, excluding the Emperor from Provence and establishing close relations with the Pope. He strengthened the administration of Provence by dividing the county into bailiwicks, where the bailiff was like a governor or prefect. The cosmopolitan nature of the Middle Ages is further indicated by the Count's appointment of an Englishman, Gervase of Tilbury, as the senior judge. Dante mentioned the outstanding legislation of Ramon Berenguer V, which even included a guarantee of safety on public highways.

Slavery existed on the Riviera for many years, particularly in Marseilles. The slaves were mostly women working in domestic service. There is an example of manumission in Provence around 960 through the ritual of a penny placed on the head *(per denarium)*.

Ramon Berenguer V died in 1245. His renown in Europe was capped by the marriages of his daughters: Margaret was married to Louis IX, King of France; Eleanor to Henry III, King of England; Sanchia to Richard, Earl of Cornwall, King of the Romans, brother of the English king; and his heiress Beatrice to Charles I, Count of Anjou, brother of the French king.

CHAPTER SIX

Angevins 1246–1481

CHARLES I, COUNT OF ANJOU

Charles I, Count of Anjou, became Count of Provence and Forcalquier by his marriage to the thirteen-year-old Beatrice. So desirable was the troubled but potentially wealthy county of Provence that there were many suitors. The brilliant wedding in Aix in January 1246 was surrounded by heavily armed guards because of the fear rivals might frustrate it. Provence had acquired as count one of the most outstanding personalities of the thirteenth century. *"This Charles was the most feared and redoubtable lord, and the most valiant in arms, and the most lofty designs, of all the kings of the house of France from Charles the Great to his own day,"* wrote a near-contemporary, Giovanni Villani.

The economy of Provence flourished under his rule. His most important asset was salt, which was recurrently important in the politics of the Riviera.

The beginning of Charles' reign was troubled. Revolt broke out while he was on the Crusades. He was captured with his brother King Louis IX. On his return he ravaged Marseilles, one of the leading culprits, and in 1252 the town submitted to his rule. Towns where he suppressed rebellions included Hyères and Grasse. He ended the consulates and installed vicars to rule the towns. Now at last, all of Provence acknowledged the suzerainty of the Count. When trouble from Marseilles bubbled up again in 1263, Charles executed twelve citizens the following year. Thereafter, Provence was in debt to Charles for a peace it had not seen for a long time. Moreover he extended his influence to nearby Piedmont and Lombardy. Nice benefited from his *excursus* into Piedmont and from an arsenal and shipyard he built in the town in 1251. In 1258 he acquired the county of Ventimiglia from its count and attached it to Nice. Charles believed in divide and rule and saw to it that most of his administrators were French, not Provençal.

The French Pope Clement IV had Charles crowned King of Sicily, of which the Pope was supreme feudal lord, on 6 January 1266. It was part of the struggle for power between the Papacy and the Holy Roman Empire. He also ruled southern Italy, the Regno, as a papal fief. The acquisition of the kingship was not without cost. Charles had to agree to pay the Pope a yearly stipend of 10,000 gold pieces, which was later reduced to 8,000. But Charles could tax the Church in France and Provence for part of the revenues for three years. To acquire the territories he had to fight a war against Manfred, illegitimate son of the Emperor Frederick II Hohenstaufen, whose army he annihilated at the Battle of Benevento on 26 February 1266. Charles defeated Manfred's nephew, the sixteen-year-old Conradin, the last of the Hohenstaufen dynasty, at the Battle of Tagliacozza in 1268, later to capture him and execute him in public in the marketplace in Naples. By purchase in 1277, Charles became King of Jerusalem.

When Louis IX, King of France died in 1270, his widow Margaret tried to wrest Provence, or her share of the county, away from Charles. Her son Philip III averted war by negotiating a settlement that left Provence in Charles' possession but assigned 2,000 livres of the income of the county to Margaret.

Provence, Marseilles and Nice in particular benefited from the wars Charles fought in Italy. Some 700 Provençal and French aristocrats became lords in the Regno and occupied the chief positions in the central administration and the royal army. In 1273 Charles imported into Italy from Provence 140 peasant families to develop the countryside with the inducement of tax breaks. Charles did not overlook the contribution of the citizens of the Riviera to his battles in Italy. On the battlefield of Tagliacozzo, he knighted a townsman from Grasse whose role in the royal victory was thought to have been outstanding. The tax privileges which went with this knighthood would have been especially appreciated when he returned home. Charles knighted Guilhem Olivari, admiral of the Nice navy, in 1269 as a reward for his assistance in the subjugation of Sicily. Provence and the Regno increasingly came together. Provençal jurisdiction came under the Great Court in Naples in 1277.

Charles wrote at least two troubadour songs when he was a young man. But between 1265 and 1268 he repressed them and in 1269 at the Council of Perugia, he forbade all singing of songs critical of himself. One of the most distinguished troubadours at this time, who was even mentioned by Dante, was Paulet of Marseilles. The poetry of the troubadours, which had been born around 1100 and was an important part of Provençal culture, died out around 1270.

The language of the troubadours was Provençal or Occitan (pronounced Oxitan). It was the language of the land where the word for 'yes' was *oc,* as opposed to the northern French *oïl,* which became *oui.* It was a Romance language, closer to Latin than French was. The French *aimer* in Occitan was *amar; savoir, saber; heure; ora.* Occitan is known by about two million people. The nineteenth-century revival of Provençal was called *Félibrige* and its most famous exponent was Frédéric Mistral.

The illustrious reign of Charles ended in disaster when in 1282 came the Sicilian Vespers. The Sicilians, resenting the Angevin rule, opened their ports to the Spaniards' Peter of Aragon. Charles' troops were beaten and two Provençal naval squadrons were annihilated. His ambitions frustrated, Charles died in Italy in 1285. In *The Divine Comedy*, Dante has Charles and Peter reconciled and singing together at the gates of Purgatory.

Angevin monarchs held on to the kingdom of Sicily until 1435, although it consisted only of southern Italy.

*

CHARLES II AND ROBERT

The successor of Charles I was his son Charles II of Salerno, King of Naples and Count of Provence and Forcalquier, who was a prisoner in Catalonia. While he was incarcerated by the Catalan-Aragonese rulers, the domains were held in joint regency by Robert II of Artois and a papal legate. In 1288 the first meeting of an Estates-General of Provence, consisting of nobles, clergy and town representatives, took place to arrange his ransom.

Charles I had sent him to govern Provence from 1279–1282. Charles II was released, leaving three of his sons and sixty Provençal and twenty Marseilles nobles as hostages. He renounced his claim to Sicily. He paid great attention to Provence, particularly in matters of religion. In 1294 he published an ordinance in Nice, which included compulsory attendance at Mass. Jews were forbidden from employing Christian servants or holding judicial posts. Naples' control over Provence was relaxed from 1296.

In 1306 Robert, Duke of Calabria, the son of Charles II and his vicar-general in Provence, introduced more anti-Jewish measures. These included one particularly absurd rule forbidding them to practice medicine, given they were almost the only doctors in Provence. The Jews appealed to Charles and gave him a large present to get him to reverse the decisions of his son. Charles not only reversed his son's measures but also improved the lot of the Jews in general.

In accordance with the papal bull of 22 November 1307, Charles arrested twenty-one Knights Templars, imprisoned them in the castle of Meyrargues and transferred their goods to the Hospitallers.

Charles II died in Naples in 1309 and was succeeded by his son Robert the Wise, Duke of Calabria, now King of Naples and Count of Provence and Forcalquier. The reign of Robert felt the full effect of the economic problems of Provence, and in particular Marseilles, which had begun under his father with the secession of Sicily and the closing of the Levant. Competition with Venice, Genoa and Montpellier, favoured by the King of France, also increased. His preoccupation with Italy meant that the liberties of cities in Provence were greatly enlarged. Robert died in 1343 after an undistinguished reign, not helped by natural disasters in Provence in the 1340s: torrential rain, floods, crop failure and famine.

During the reigns of Charles II and Robert, the papacy was based in France, established in Avignon from 1305. It moved back to Rome in 1377 but from 1378 to 1417, there were popes in both Avignon and Rome. Indeed, from 1409 there were three popes. In 1417, the Council of Constance dismissed all three pontiffs and acclaimed Martin V as the sole pope in their place.

*

JOAN I, QUEEN OF NAPLES

Robert's successor, his granddaughter, the beautiful Joan I, Queen of Naples and Countess of Provence and Forcalquier, who was aged seventeen, more than made up for his dullness. Joan was crowned by the Pope as Queen of Naples on 28 August 1344. She held her Italian territories by the grace of the papacy and quarrelled much with it over her powers. She was suspected of complicity in the murder of her first husband, Prince Andrew of the Hungarian branch of the House of Anjou in 1345, whom she had married when they were both small children. However, no evidence was ever produced to prove her guilt. He was strangled with a cord and flung from a window with a rope tied to his genitals. Joan married thrice more amidst great intrigues and fighting. Two years after the death of Andrew, she married her cousin Louis of Taranto, who had probably been responsible for the murder. Louis filled the administration with his clients and friends and antagonised powerful interests in Naples. They included the influential house of Les Baux, two of whose members were killed resisting him.

Louis King of Hungary invaded Italy in 1347 to avenge the death of his brother Andrew. Joan fled to Provence by Provençal-owned galleys on 15 January 1348. Her husband Louis of Taranto followed the next day. Meantime, after a convivial dinner, Louis King of Hungary had his guest Charles of Durazzo, one of the suspects in the murder of his brother, beheaded in exactly the same spot as where Andrew had been murdered. The bloody trunk of his body was thrown over the balcony railing into the garden below, where Andrew's corpse had lain.

The Hungarians took the two-year-old son of Joan, Charles Martel, to Hungary where he soon died from the strain of the journey.

Joan was welcomed in Marseilles, where she was known as 'Mistress of Marseilles', but not in Avignon, where she met the Pope. Joan's actions alienated some of Provence. She handed over her rights in Gattières to the Bishop of Vence and Eze and La Turbie to the Grimaldis of Monaco. However, in Aix she swore on 19 February to appoint only persons native to Provence to the government. The local authorities and aristocracy immediately responded with an oath of fealty, so all was sweetness and light.

Joan had an audience in Avignon with the Pope, who declared her innocent of complicity in the murder of Andrew. She needed money to secure her return to Naples so pawned Avignon to the pope. She had already pawned her crown, which she was now able to redeem. She was not going to go back to Naples without her crown. A combination of circumstances, including the plague, caused Louis of Hungary to abandon Italy on 24 May 1348 and return to Hungary, although most of his army stayed.

*

The plague of 1348 was notable. The year 541 had seen the first of the great plagues to strike the Mediterranean. It was called the Plague of Justinian, or the First Great Pandemic and periodically returned. The Second Great Pandemic of 1348 spread from Marseilles to the rest of western Europe and returned about every six to ten years until the late fifteenth century. One study of 7,655 householders in Provence gives a mortality rate of 52 per cent. In 1315–16, Provence had a population of about 400,000, but only 150,000 after a period of recovery in 1471. Paradoxically, by reducing the population, the deaths from the plagues did something to relieve the famines of the fourteenth century. The shortage of labour meant that feudal lords were unable to enforce their traditional rights and serfdom became irrelevant.

The plague of 1348 was the greatest demographic disaster Europe suffered in its history. The poet Guillaume de Machaut, who lived through it, said death *"leapt from its cage"*, attacking its victims suddenly and indiscriminately. The German Max Planck Institute has determined from DNA samples that a single strain of plague bacteria sparked both the plague of 1348 and modern pandemics.

In the epidemic of 1407, Nice lost nearly 8,000 inhabitants and St-Laurent-du-Var, La Gaude, Auribeau and La Napoule were entirely depopulated. In 1580, two-thirds of the citizens of Nice perished and again in 1631 there were 10,000 victims in the county. Convicts from Villefranche were brought in to bury the dead.

The general belief was that the plagues came through the air, not by contagion and were inflicted by God because of sin in the community. Those considered sinful, such as Jews, prostitutes and homosexuals were therefore persecuted.

The last great plague came to the Riviera in 1720 and particularly desolated Marseilles, where 50 per cent of the population died.

*

Joan and Louis of Taranto returned to Italy, as did Louis of Hungary. The attempt to regain their kingdom from the Hungarians had mixed results, but Louis of Hungary finally left Italy in October 1350, never to return. On Christmas Day 1356, Joan regained Sicily.

Jean le Bon, King of France wanted to be Joan's husband number three, after the death of Louis of Taranto from the plague in 1362, in order to unite France and Provence. But he did not succeed because the Pope Urban V was able to veto it, which he did. Although he was French, he thought the absorption of Provence by France would be a threat to papal independence.

The Pope did not veto James IV titular king of Majorca as the third husband. He had been imprisoned for almost fourteen years by his uncle, King Peter of Aragon in an iron cage. Not surprisingly, he was mentally deranged. After the death of James in 1376 Joan married the military adventurer, Otto of Brunswick.

Joan's adoption in 1380 of Louis of Anjou-Provence, brother of Charles V, King of France, and her nomination of him as her successor, divided Provence. There was now a second house of Anjou. On the one hand were Louis' supporters led by Marseilles and Arles, and including on the Riviera La Ciotat and Cassis. On the other hand were supporters of her cousin and nephew Charles of Durazzo, led by Aix, Nice and Tarascon. Fighting continued until 1386.

Provence was not a party to the Hundred Years' War between France and England, but felt its repercussions. From 1357 Joan's reign had been marked by the armed bands, including Englishmen, left over from the war who pillaged the Riviera countryside. Notable among the French was Arnaud de Cervole, called the 'Archpriest' because of the clerical benefice he had once held. He cheekily called his band *Società dell'Acquisto* (Company of Acquisition). His contemporaries called it the 'Great Company'. He teamed up with Raymond des Baux to form a band of 2,000 men. Pope Innocent VI was so scared of Cervole in Avignon that he invited him to dinner, gave him a pardon for all his sins and 40,000 écus to leave the area.

In 1357, local bands loyal to Raymond des Baux seized Brignoles and burnt Draguignan. St-Maximin-la-Ste-Baume was sacked. It was an important town because it claimed to possess the tomb of Mary Magdalene, who was reputed to have fled there from the Holy Land in a miraculous boat with neither rudder nor sail. Crowds of refugees abandoned the open country and took refuge within the walls of Marseilles and Toulon. But so active were the defenders of Marseilles that the Archpriest abandoned his plan to sack it. He moved north: Marseilles had saved Provence. That revolt eventually fizzled out and Raymond des Baux ended up in prison. But the Great Company came back in 1361 and 1365 and was bought off by the Pope. In 1366, the Archpriest had a row with some of his men and they murdered him. In February 1368 another *routier*, Bertrand du Guesclin invaded, but the campaign ended inconclusively.

*

CIVIL WAR

In 1381, the Pope of Rome, Urban VI dethroned Joan and gave the kingdom to Charles of Durazzo under the title of Charles III. Charles had Joan assassinated in 1382. Chroniclers differ on the method: starvation, poison, strangulation, smothering. Her corpse was exposed in the Naples cathedral for six days before burial in a deep well, so that there was no doubt surrounding her death.

Civil war broke out in Provence on the news of the death of Joan. The Avignon Pope Clement VII, the seneschal Foulque d'Agoult, French troops and Marseilles supported Louis I. Supporting communes on the Riviera included Grasse. Aix led a union supporting Charles of

Durazzo, called 'The Union of Aix'. The union included Nice, Tarascon, Draguignan, Fréjus, Grimaud, Hyères, Toulon, Puget, Lorgues, St-Paul-de-Vence, St-Maximin, Barcelonnette, Signes and Ventimiglia.

Louis I of Anjou-Provence was crowned King of Naples, Sicily, and Jerusalem, including Provence, by Pope Clement in 1383. Thus began the duplication of the kings of Naples, since Charles III already had that title. Accompanied by Amadeo, the 'green count' of Savoy, who soon died in an epidemic, Louis invaded Lombardy on his way to southern Italy. But he was outwitted by Charles of Durazzo. His army wasted away in the heel of Italy for a year and a half and he died in 1384 from a severe chill, caught after overexerting himself against looters in his army.

Charles of Durazzo, crowned King of Hungary as Charles II, became embroiled in quarrels in Hungary, and was assassinated in prison in Buda in 1386.

The deaths of the protagonists soon moved the fight to the next generation. In 1389 the antipope Clement VII invested Louis II of Anjou-Provence, the son of Louis I, as King of Naples and Count of Provence and Forcalquier. This was the second titular duplication. (He had been recognised as Count of Provence in 1387.) He was aged twelve, but his mother Marie de Blois vigorously fought for his interests. The investiture took place in the presence of King Charles VI of France, underlining the dependence of Provence on France. In 1409 he abandoned Pope Benedict XIII and recognised the antipope Alexander V, who named him King of Naples yet again. All Provence submitted to Louis except Nice, the bailiwick of Puget-Théniers, the Val de Lantosque and the bailiwick of Barcelonnette, which in 1388 had handed themselves over to the neighbouring Count of Savoy. He had then promptly moved to occupy the valley of the Ubaye and left bank of the Var. French troops left Provence in exchange for an indemnity.

The status of Savoy had changed in 1361 when the Emperor Charles IV had succeeded in bringing Savoy under imperial sovereignty. The counts of Savoy were raised to dukes in 1416, and in 1536 removed their residence from Chambéry to Turin in Piedmont.

Louis tried to revive the countryside of Provence, encouraging immigration from northern Italy. But during much of his reign the inhabitants of Provence had to contend with the continued depredations of Arnaud de Cervole and Raymond Roger de Beaufort, Viscount of Turenne. Communes on the Riviera that particularly suffered included Cabris, Auribeau, Mouans-Sartoux, Vallauris, Biot, Valbonne, St-Laurent-du-Var and Glandèves. Wolves and bears returned to the desolated area.

For nine years from 1390, Louis fought in Italy to try to recover his throne in Naples. He returned to Provence in 1399 and subsequently made two more expeditions to Italy, but gave up in 1411 and died in Angers in 1417.

Ladislaus the Magnanimous succeeded his father Charles of Durazzo as King of Naples and Count of Provence and Forcalquier in 1386, at the age of nine. His mother Margaret of Durazzo acted as regent. He successfully fought off Louis II in Italy and died in 1414.

In a campaign financed by the States of Provence, Louis II's successor, Louis III from 1420 tried to seize the Naples throne, with which the Roman Pope Martin V had invested him in 1419, from Joan II, Queen of Naples, sister and successor of Ladislaus, and Alfonso of Aragon, but without success. Louis never visited Provence, but the Aragonese, against whom he fought, sacked Marseilles in 1423. The Aragonese admiral seized the chain that formed its chief defence and carried it away as a trophy. The navies of Aragon and Marseilles fought until they made a truce in 1431. Provence saw a mixture of rulers in the absence of Louis, the most important of which were his mother, Yolande of Aragon and later his brother, Charles of Maine. Louis died in 1434.

The insecurity caused by the fifty years of civil war from 1337 to 1388 hampered travel and disrupted agriculture with cultivated areas neglected. Villages were deserted. Cities changed, with open suburbs abandoned and convents put behind walls. One benefit was the increase in sheep-farming.

*

'GOOD KING' RENÉ

Like his one-time predecessor, Charles II, René of Anjou who followed his brother Louis III, started his reign in prison. By marriage he had acquired the titles of Duke of Bar and Duke of Lorraine. While fighting to secure his domains he was imprisoned by the Duke of Burgundy, who only released him in 1436 after payment of a large ransom. Financed by the states of Provence, he tried unsuccessfully from 1436 to 1442 to conquer his Italian kingdom and thereafter until 1467 other parts of Italy. René fought the English alongside his brother-in-law Charles VII, King of France, but a truce resulted in his daughter Marguerite marrying the English King Henry VI.

In 1442 René returned to Provence. It was the end of the kingdom of Naples for the Angevins. The year 1444 was important for Marseilles. In that year Jacques Coeur, a wealthy merchant, settled there and relaunched the spice trade with the Levant. From 1447 to 1450 René resided in Provence, where his main preoccupation was fending off the incursions of the Aragonese. His activities later included fighting the English again. René had spent only about 10 per cent of his reign in Provence. He died in 1480 and only long after his death did he acquire the sobriquet of 'Good King René'. The people of Provence would not have given him that title while he was ruling them and demanding high taxes. He was famous for loving roses, charities and his subjects. He wrote and perhaps painted. He built a tunnel under Mount Viso as part of his efforts to increase trade. Unfortunately for a ruler of Provence, he hated olive oil. He tended to favour giving jobs to Frenchmen, rather than Provençaux. Some historians consider Provence flourished under his rule, but others believe any prosperity was merely a catching-up exercise. *"If the people are richer, the royal treasury is bigger,"* he said. The number of households roughly tripled between 1470 and 1540.

His cousin Charles III of Anjou briefly succeeded him in Provence on 10 July 1480. But Provence was already slipping into the orbit of France. When René II of Lorraine invaded Provence with a small army in 1481, Charles was only saved by the intervention of the French King Louis XI, who wanted to get his hands on Provence, with 18,000 lancers.

After recapturing Forcalquier the war became for Charles a triumphal progress through the Riviera, where he visited Draguignan, Trans-en-Provence, Roquebrune, Fréjus, les Arcs, Toulon and Marseilles, where he was welcomed as the triumphant conqueror of René II.

Looking at the account books of Charles III today it is not surprising that France would soon take over Provence. At the moment that he was asking the towns of the region to rally for the war, he was wasting the public revenues on frivolous clothes for his bastards and entourage. He bought taffeta, damascene, velvet and silk. Louis XI, on the other hand, was renowned for his austerity. Charles spent over 1,000 florins, whereas to equip 100 soldiers cost only 121 florins. He bought elaborate new clothes for all for the entry into Marseilles.

Charles fell ill as soon as he entered Marseilles. He ate only game, fish, fruit and vegetables. Fine wine was brought from Aix. He spent 63 florins on medicines.

Extravagance was not confined to the lay monarchy. In 1460 Pope Pius II published a draft bull on clerical behaviour. Cardinals created before Pius II became pope in 1458 were not to have more than sixty servants and forty teams of horses. Those created by Pius II were to have no more than twenty servants and four teams of horses. Curial members were to get rid of frivolous members of their households, to expel concubines and loose women. Any curial official found consorting with a prostitute was to be fined heavily.

On 10 December 1481 in Marseilles, Charles signed his will leaving Provence to his cousin Louis XI, King of France, but not without recommending the conservation of all the privileges, rights, franchises and statutes of Provence and the maintenance of its customs. Charles died the next day. Provence was now French.

CHAPTER SEVEN

French Provence and Savoyard Nice 1481–1598

KING OF FRANCE AND COUNT OF PROVENCE AND FORCALQUIER

Louis XI, the King of France ruled in Provence from 1481 as 'Count of Provence and Forcalquier'. Provence was regarded as beyond the national frontier. Significant in the letters patent, which the king signed on 19 December 1481, was the statement that he acquired Provence by hereditary right. He thus showed that he regarded the will of Charles merely as confirmation. Historians have argued over the significance of the clause in the marriage contract between Charles I of Anjou and Beatrice, which assured the union of Provence with the crown in the event of no male successor.

Provence had been independent from France for 602 years, dating from 879 when Boso was elected King of Provence. Louis XI was the 28th Count of Provence.

The Lord of Soliès, Palamède de Forbin, a member of a rich family of Marseilles traders, who had persuaded Charles of Anjou to leave the county to the King, got his reward with the post of governor. He had the full powers of the sovereign. He did not fail to appoint his relatives to the most lucrative offices.

Eighteen days after the death of Charles, the Estates of Provence declared allegiance to the King of France. The assembly met on 15 January 1482 and approved sixty-five demands, which they presented to Forbin. Then, together with many other citizens, raising their right hands, thrice they cried "Vive le roi". The demands and requests for the constitution of Provence included:

- Retain all previous laws and constitutions.
- Maintain judicial independence. This gave citizens of Provence greater rights than those of the rest of France.
- Public offices to be held only by natives.
- Aix to continue as the capital.
- Maintain existing agreements with Savoy, Genoa, Avignon and the Comtat Venaissin.
- Get the prince of Monaco to suppress harmful rights affecting trade with Italy.

The king accepted all the demands and requests.

He later heeded the complaints of the inhabitants of Provence about Forbin's abuses and effectively replaced him in 1483 with a commissioner extraordinary, Jean Baudricourt, who was honest and corrected many of the injustices. But that did not stop the replacement in offices of many citizens of Provence with Frenchmen despite the agreements of 1482. Reliable men were placed in charge of the key fortress towns of Toulon, Castellane, Fréjus and Lambesc. The fortifications of Toulon were destroyed and Forcalquier, Grasse and Draguignan occupied by troops. Using what in later years were called the 'salami tactics' of communists in acquiring power, he attenuated the rights of the citizens of Provence.

Louis XI died in 1483 and was succeeded by his son Charles VIII, a minor. His elder sister Anne de Beaujeu was proclaimed regent and Charles did not enter into personal rule until 1491. The regent partly reversed the policies of Louis XI and restored many posts to natives of Provence. They included the vicarages of Grasse and Draguignan. In accordance with the demand of the Estates, the monarchy agreed to an act of equality between Provence and France in letters patent of 4 October 1486, accepted by the Estates on 9 April 1487. But there was no longer a reference to the principal officers being natives of Provence.

Louis XII succeeded to the throne in 1498, Francis I in 1515, Henri II in 1547 and Francis II in 1559.

In 1535 the edicts of Joinville and Is-sur-Tille limited the scope of the old institutions of the Estates and the seneschal and increased that of the *parlement* of Aix (which had been established in 1501–02) in justice and the governor in administration. In 1539, the ordinance of Villers-Cotterêts laid down that judicial acts should in future be in French and not Latin. This measure ushered in a long period of bilingualism, with the elite using French and the masses Provençal.

*

WAR

Provence was drawn into the rivalry between the Habsburg Empire and France in 1524 when the army of Charles V crossed the River Var and seized Toulon and Aix. The area had gravely suffered from the plague in 1521 and now it had to bear the ravages of the French, who pursued a scorched earth policy with the crops. The union with France cost it dear. Marseilles showed itself as very different from Toulon and Aix, with the Marseilles ladies of high society joining with the ladies of the streets to build fortifications to withstand a siege, which lasted forty-one days. Honoré de Puget had his head cut off for having given the keys of Aix to the enemy. The imperial troops withdrew across the Var. In 1525 the French King Francis I was captured by the imperialists at the Battle of Pavia and he was not released until the following year. Francis invaded Italy in 1536 and seized Barcelonnette, Savoy and Piedmont. The Duke of Savoy was left only with Nice. He took refuge in the castle with his wife, his son, his companions and his archives.

After a truce Charles V invaded Provence again in 1536, announcing that he was going to take possession of 'his' county. Provence saw the horrors of war when Charles hanged all the citizens who had hidden in the Tour du Muy. They had planned to assassinate Charles, but made a mistake and killed one of his friends instead. After a siege of a few days, Charles promised them their lives if they would surrender, which they did. He then hanged them all.

After a spell in an undefended Aix where he had himself proclaimed King of Provence, Charles V again unsuccessfully besieged Marseilles. His retreat to Italy was a disaster in which his troops were attacked by the peasants of the area and where he left 20,000 dead.

History repeated itself with a truce in 1538 mediated by Pope Paul III in Nice. The Pope wanted to stay in the castle, but Nice refused and he had to make do with the convent of Ste-Croix, site of the present Croix de Marbre, outside the city. Accompanied by 1,600 cavalry and 6,000 infantry, Francis set himself up in the castle of Villeneuve-Loubet and Charles on his galley, the *Saint-Jage* off Villefranche. Such was their mutual animosity, the monarchs did not meet and on 18 June 1538, the truce was signed by their representatives. In the Syrian negotiations in Geneva in 2016 such arm's-length diplomacy was called 'proximity talks'.

When war resumed in 1542 – six years before the truce was due to end – France exploited to the full the strengths of the new Ottoman ally it had acquired in 1536. The Turkish admiral Hayreddin Barbarossa's great fleet of 150 ships sailed into Marseilles harbour on 20 July 1543 with much pomp. With the French fleet, they headed for Villefranche where they arrived on 5 August. The locals fled either to Genoa or into the mountains. The attackers besieged Nice, surrounding it with heavy cannon which had deadly effect. The washerwoman Catherine Ségurane was the heroine of the siege. She is reputed to have seized an enemy standard by knocking out its bearer with the stick with which she beat her washing. With cries of *"Victory, Victory"*, she rallied the citizens. One story, which may or may not be true, is that she stood on the ramparts and exposed her large bottom to the enemy below.

The shocked Janissaries beat a retreat. The French set fire to the lower town. The Turks repaired to Toulon to pass the winter. The decision, which involved the deportation of most of the local population, the commandeering of property for the Ottoman officers, and the establishment of Muslim institutions including a mosque and a slave market, outraged European public opinion, and caused a great deal of unease in France as well. The experience probably had some resonance in the subsequent powerful religious tensions in Provence.

Peace came in 1544 with the treaty of Crépy.

The mid-sixteenth century saw a recurrence of piracy, which had been long endemic, emanating from many sources. The islands of Lérins particularly suffered. On 30 May 1400, pirates from Genoa attacked.

In 1414 the Saracens; in 1423 the Aragonese. From 1441 to 1455, the Catalans attacked almost every year. Pirates from Nice and Monaco attacked Antibes, Cannes and La Napoule. In 1560, after having burnt down Roquebrune, 500 Barbary pirates attacked the nearby coast and the soldiers of Duke Emmanuel Philibert had to retreat towards Villefranche, leaving behind imprisoned men, for whom they later had to pay ransoms for their release.

*

WARS OF RELIGION

The south of Provence experienced its most noteworthy event in the run-up to the Wars of Religion in Draguignan (in what is now the Var) in 1559. In Castellane the nobles, brothers Antoine and Paulon de Mauvans, appointed a Protestant pastor, which caused the Catholics to rise up. There was much politicking involving Paris and Aix, but Antoine began a campaign of terror and murdered seven priests in a well near Barjols. The de Mauvans organised a demonstration in Draguignan, which was attacked by the mob. Antoine de Mauvans and the provost were murdered. Parts of Antoine de Mauvans' body were sent for exhibition in Aix. Paulon exacted vengeance in Draguignan.

The Wars of Religion between Protestants and Catholics, which raged across France from 1562 to 1629, were fought particularly fiercely in the south because of the strength of the Protestants, who increasingly became known by their opponents as Huguenots. The sympathies of the monarchy swung between the two factions as it tried to manage both sides to preserve its independence. In 1562 Catherine de' Medici, the regent of her son Charles IX, who had succeeded his brother in 1560, promulgated a first edict of toleration. The first consul of Aix, Pontevès-Flassans, got a gang together and massacred the Protestant population of Tourves, a village north of Toulon. The Count of Crussol and the Count of Tende pursued him to Barjols and, after a siege of several days, this time more than 600 Catholics had their throats cut. Pontevès-Flassans escaped

1. Bronze Age rock carving known as the Sorcerer from the Vallée des Merveilles (Valley of Marvels), Tende, Alpes-Maritimes. His raised hands each brandishes a dagger blade. Guide reference: Z VIII GII R3 [4] No. 12.

The Vallée des Merveilles holds one of the largest quantities of open-air Bronze Age petroglyphs in Europe.

It is part of the Mercantour National Park and the rock engravings are mainly to be found in two valleys, Merveilles and Fontanalba.

2. The Treasury of Massalia (the Greek name of Marseilles) at Delphi in Greece, probably centre left. Its presence there, built around 540BC, is an indicator of the wealth of Massalia not long after its foundation. Not more than seven or eight Greek cities had treasuries at Delphi. The founders of Marseilles in about 600BC were Greeks from the city of Phocaea on the Aegean coast of modern Turkey.

3. Cimiez, the Roman Cemelenum, to the north of Nice, was the capital of the province of the Alpes Maritimae. The huge northern baths shown here were for the high-ranking Romans and are one of the best preserved examples anywhere in the former Roman empire. Embrun replaced Cimiez as the capital of the province in 284. Cimiez can be visited and has a museum.

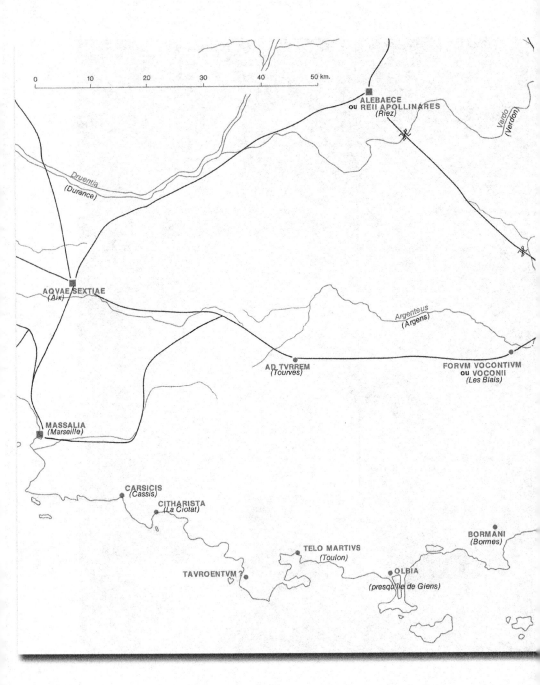

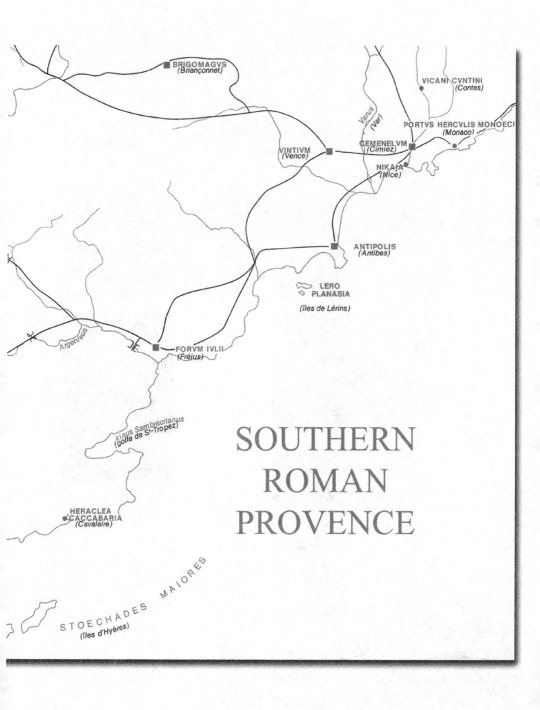

BRIGOMAGVS
(Briançonnet)

VICANI CVNTINI
(Contes)

Varus
(Var)

PORTVS HERCVLIS MONOECI
(Monaco)

VINTIVM
(Vence)

CEMENELVM
(Cimiez)

NIKAIA
(Nice)

ANTIPOLIS
(Antibes)

LERO
PLANASIA

(îles de Lérins)

Argenteus

sinus Sambracitanus
(golfe de St-Tropez)

FORVM IVLII
(Fréjus)

SOUTHERN
ROMAN
PROVENCE

HERACLEA
CACCABARIA
(Cavalaire)

STOECHADES MAIORES
(îles d'Hyères)

5. TOP: The monastery of the Ile St-Honorat, off the coast of Cannes, was founded by St. Honoratus in 410. The island and monastery can be visited by ferry from Cannes.

6. FAR RIGHT: On the death of King Clovis in 511 Gaul was divided among his four sons Clothar, Theuderic, Childebert and Chlodomer.

7. RIGHT: A gold solidus coin of the Frankish king Theudebert I. It would have circulated in what we now call the Riviera, which was ruled by Childebert.

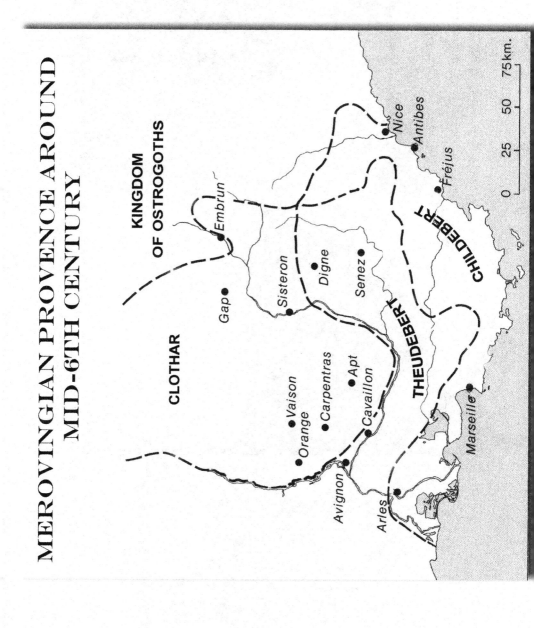

MEROVINGIAN PROVENCE AROUND
MID-6TH CENTURY

KINGDOM
OF OSTROGOTHS

CLOTHAR

Gap

Embrun

Sisteron

Digne

Senez

Vaison

Orange

Carpentras

Apt

Cavaillon

Avignon

Arles

THEUDEBERT

CHILDEBERT

Marseille

Nice

Antibes

Fréjus

Marseille

0   25   50   75 km.

11. Prince Andrew (1327–1345) was first husband of Joan I queen of Naples. He was murdered by defenestration.

10. Charles I Count of Anjou (1227–1285), youngest son of King Louis VIII of France. He became king of Sicily and also ruled southern Italy.

9. Margaret of Provence (1221–1295) was eldest daughter of Ramon Berenguer V Count of Provence whose wife Beatrice of Savoy produced a remarkable family of four girls who all married monarchs. Margaret was queen of King Louis IX of France and accompanied him on crusade.

12. LEFT: Chapelle St Clair in Venanson, Alpes Maritimes, containing this fresco was built in the 15th Century to give protection from the plague.

13. RIGHT: A tournament organised around 1460 by Good King René of Anjou (1409-80), a favourite hobby of the monarch.

14. Charles V and Francis I shaking hands after signing the Truce of Nice in 1538, Pope Paul III, who had been mediator, benignly looking on. In fact the monarchs never met in the truce negotiations.

16. ABOVE: King Louis XIV eventually won the civil war of the Fronde and celebrated his victory as Jupiter.

17. RIGHT: The entrance to the hotel where Thomas Jefferson stayed in Nice when he was American minister in Paris. The building, which can be entered, was on place St-Dominique, now 5 rue de la Préfecture.

15. BELOW: A fine renaissance window in Rougiers, Var. On either side of the window are two cupids.

20. BELOW: An Italian cartoon of Emperor Napoleon III celebrating his acquisition of Nice and Savoy in 1860. Napoleon throws a bone to Austria-Hungary. The Ottoman sultan is in the centre. Also present are King Victor Emmanuel, Count Cavour and Guiseppe Garibaldi.

18. ABOVE: The Count of Mirabeau was the most important leader of the French Revolution in the Midi. Here he is shown on 23rd June 1789 defying in the Assembly the king's command to disperse.

19. RIGHT: The church of the village of Opio, Alpes-Maritimes, which provided the first clerical martyr from the diocese in the French Revolution.

La Reine d'Angleterre à Nice

21. ABOVE: The French appreciated the boost to tourism from Queen Victoria's nine visits to the Riviera. But this anti-British postcard was published when the Fashoda incident in 1898 almost led to war.

22. RIGHT: The American dancer Josephine Baker dressed in bananas. Her summer visits to the Riviera helped to make the region fashionable in the summer.

23. LEFT: Identity card of the Combat resistance in the south of France in 1944. The holder was in military region R2, which included the Riviera.

24. Operation Dragoon on 15th August 1944 when Americans, British and French landed on the Riviera from North Africa.

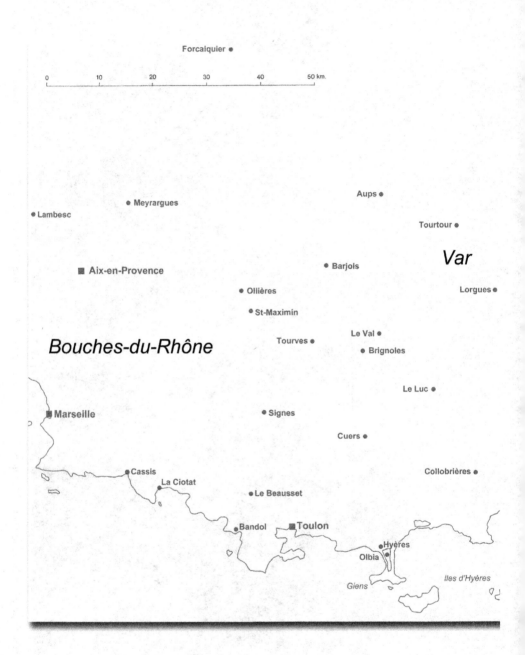

Puget-Théniers ●

Alpes-Maritimes

Sospel ●

Italie

Escarène ●

Bordighera ●
Menton ●
Roquebrune-Cap-Martin ●

Tourrettes-Levens ●
● Vence

■ Monaco
● Beaulieu-sur-Mer

Escragnolles ●

Gourdon ●
St-Paul-de-Vence ●

Nice ■ ● Villefranche

Magagnosc ●
Grasse ■ ● Opio

● St-Laurent-du-Var

Cabris ●

● Valbonne

● Cagnes
● Villeneuve-Loubet

Sophia-Antipolis ●
Mouans-Sartoux ●

Fayence ●
Bargemon ● ● ● Montauroux
Tourrettes

● Mougins

Vallauris ●
Le Cannet ●
Cannes ■

■ Antibes
● Juan-les-Pins

Cap d'Antibes

● Draguignan

La Napoule ●
Théoule-sur-Mer ●

Iles de Lérins

● Trans-en-Provence

Les Arcs ● ● Le Muy

Fréjus ■ ● St-Raphael

Méditerranée

● La Garde-Freinet

Grimaud ●
■ St-Tropez

FRENCH
RiVIERA

26. When the town of Fréjus in the Var needed a new stadium in the twenty-first century the authorities did not waste money starting from scratch. Instead, not without heated accusations of philistinism, it refurbished the amphitheatre the Romans had built in the second century. Fréjus was an important Roman military base.

to Porquerolles. Revenge came three months later when in Fréjus, the Catholic mob killed René de Cipières, son of the Count of Tende, and twenty-six of his companions.

In 1563, Charles attained his majority and the following year he and his mother embarked on a tour of the kingdom, which included Toulon, Hyères and Marseilles.

Towards 1568–1570, Jews were driven out of the towns of Provence, but were received amicably in Savoy.

A period of relative calm followed the royal tour in Provence and the area escaped repercussions from the St Bartholomew massacre of the Protestants in Paris on 24 August 1572. The governor Sommerive and the Count of Carcès, Lieutenant General and chief of the Catholics, refused to allow anything comparable to take place in Provence.

The death of Charles IX and the succession of Henry III were followed by changes in the governing elite: Sommerive/Tende had already been replaced by the Maréchal de Tavannes in 1572, but Henry in turn replaced Tavannes by Albert de Gondi, Count of Retz, as governor, who immediately fell out with Carcès, the Lieutenant General of the province and the governor's immediate subordinate. The tensions between Retz and Carcès played themselves out from 1574 onwards, encouraging local violence, skirmishes and a small war, which climaxed in the revolts and violence of 1578–79. The structure of provincial government had been undermined since the mid-1570s by the personal rivalry at the top.

In what was supposed to be a period of peace, in April 1579 a band of peasants secretly assembled and massacred 600 dependants of Carcès in the village of Cuers, north of Toulon. At about the same time, another group of peasants in the village of Callas near Draguignan sacked the chateau of the local seigneur, which set off looting and burning of the nobles' properties and the inhabitants were forced to flee for safety. The peasants, known as Razas, who were half-shaven, were both Protestants and Catholics. The population had other thoughts than war in 1580 when a ship docked in Cannes that carried the plague, from which many died.

On 15 June 1584 François, Duke of Alençon and Anjou, brother of Charles and Henry, died. That made Henry of Navarre, a Protestant, heir presumptive to the throne. With one blow, the conflicts broke out again, but this time the rebels became royalists. In Provence Hubert de Garde, seigneur de Vins, nephew of Carcès, took up the leadership of the Catholic League. In April 1589 the *parlement* of Aix swore allegiance to the Catholic League. In July the small royalist minority in the *parlement* withdrew to Pertuis. Marseilles rallied to the League. So now there were two Provences. Division and turmoil followed the assassination of Henry III in August. Few recognised Henry IV as king. Hubert de Vins besieged Grasse and was killed outside the town in November.

In 1590, Savoy became involved in the Wars of Religion. The Duke of Savoy, Charles-Emmanuel I headed an army of the Catholic League and the Spanish and invaded Provence, seizing St-Paul, Grasse and Aix. The *parlement* of Aix handed to him military command of Provence. Charles de Casaulx, also a leader of the Catholic League, seized power in Marseilles and repulsed attacks by Charles-Emmanuel. By March 1592 Charles-Emmanuel was forced to retreat to Nice. In August he occupied Antibes and Cannes, although the French soon took them back.

The Lieutenant-General of Provence, Bernard Nogaret de La Valette was killed outside Roquebrune in February 1592, which led to continued divided rule. The king sent his brother Jean-Louis de Nogaret de Valette, the Duke of Epernon to Provence as governor in 1593. To set an example, the Duke seized the village of Montauroux, north of Fréjus, which was held by a corps of Leaguers. He hanged all the officers and sixty soldiers.

In mid-August 1593, Provence received the news of the abjuration from Protestantism of Henry IV. *"Paris is well worth a Mass,"* he said. Widespread recognition soon followed the abjuration. Casaulx, who with the support of Spain had ruled Marseilles as an independent state, was assassinated in 1596. French troops entered Marseilles. *"I was not a king of France till now,"* Henry said when he heard the news. However, the real beneficiary of the end of the civil wars in Provence was not the king, but the Guise-Lorraine family. Playing on their links to Provence before the French monarchy assumed sovereignty, and acting as nominal royalists, it was Charles de Lorraine, Duke of Guise who spearheaded the overthrow of the Marseilles 'republic', and who had earlier coordinated the humiliating expulsion of the Duke of Epernon from the governorship in 1594. The reward for this had been the governorship, which he held with virtual autonomy from the crown until 1631.

The historian Fernand Braudel says that Provence at this time could be seen as a microcosm of France: with inflation, terrible poverty in town and countryside, the spread of brigandage and the political ruthlessness of the nobility.

Conflict with Spain, always hoping to seize Marseilles, ended with the Peace of Vervins in 1598.

The Edict of Nantes of 1598, giving freedom of conscience and certain rights of worship to the Protestants, ended the eighth War of Religion.

Historians differ on the effects of the wars in the south of France. Some cite the estimates of a commentator in Lorgues as late as 1605, which showed that of the 500 families living there, 300 were reduced to begging, 150 lived from day-to-day and 25 were overwhelmed by debt. Nonetheless in Basse-Provence the olive oil was still exported and in the ports of Avignon, Arles, Marseilles and Toulon industries of tannery, pottery, silk, paper and soap appeared.

Marseilles was especially different from the rest of Provence. Its prosperity is shown by the increase in its population, which grew from around 15,000 inhabitants in 1515 to 40,000 at the end of the century.

CHAPTER EIGHT

The Coming of Absolute Monarchy 1598–1787

WARS AND CONFLICT

In 1596, Henry IV had sent his friend Guillaume du Vair to Marseilles as president of the Chambre de Justice and in 1599 added the role of first president of the Parlement d'Aix. His first task was to clear out from Berre the troops of Savoy who still occupied it. Then he had to put down two revolts: one in 1601 by Maurice de l'Isle, a former friend of Casaulx, who was executed, and in 1605 by Louis d'Algonia, lord of Meyrargues, seemingly supported by the King of Spain, who wanted to get his hands on Marseilles. Meyrargues was also executed and his head displayed on a stake in Marseilles.

Nice felt the repercussions of war when France occupied Savoy. In 1600 the Duke of Guise attacked Nice, which valiantly defended itself. Peace came in 1601 but the French again invaded Savoy in 1629 and occupied the Nice countryside. In the years between the wars the ruler of Savoy, Charles Emmanuel I, benefited the region by building the road of the Col de Tende, improved the ports of Nice, Villefranche and St-Hospice and gave them free port status and tax advantages. He added to Nice courts, a senate and a university.

There was repeated conflict between the crown and Provence, particularly in Marseilles, over taxes and the price of salt, notably in 1630, 1631 and 1648, which usually ended in compromise. Only under Louis XIV was Provence totally integrated into the kingdom. Between 1635 and 1660 there were 282 popular risings in France as a whole. Between 1635 and 1647, there were 46 in Provence.

But René Pillorget, who has specialised in the study of seventeenth-century insurrection in Provence, emphasises that there was no peasant war in Provence between 1598 and 1635.

One of the priorities of Cardinal Richelieu, who became minister for the new King Louis XIII in 1624, was to expand the navy and the fortifications on the Mediterranean. By 1642 Toulon accommodated ninety warships, almost the whole of the navy. Giens and the Iles d'Hyères were fortified. During the Thirty Years' War in 1635, the Spanish seized the Iles de Lérins, off Cannes, and threatened Marseilles, and only in 1637 did the militias of Provence recapture them. Those militias, consisting of two men per household, were decisive in defending the coastal towns like St-Tropez.

France was preoccupied by the incursions of the Algerian pirates, who in particular attacked the coast of the Riviera and peace was not agreed until 1628.

Louis XIV succeeded to the throne at the age of five in 1643. His mother Anne became regent. The effect of the minority in Provence was that some towns like Marseilles were emboldened to challenge the authority of the monarchy.

*

FRONDES

The first of the Frondes broke out in Paris when the Paris mob rose up on 26 August 1648. It was to have great consequences for Provence and its capital, Aix. *Fronde* means slingshot and one broke the window of the carriage of Cardinal Mazarin, the king's minister, against whom much of the Frondes were targeted. Mazarin was Italian and to the xenophobic French of the seventeenth century, being Italian meant being untrustworthy, over-sexed, infected with venereal disease, or homosexual. The Fronde also resulted from the attack by the monarchy on the rights of the Paris *parlements*, which were law courts, not legislatures as in the principal functions of a British Parliament. The main point at issue was the level of taxes demanded by the war with Spain. The people of

Paris identified themselves with the interests of the *parlements*. The tax collectors, or 'snakes' as they were known, went on strike.

Provence was one of the few provinces that had its own *parlement*. There was a history of conflict between the crown and the chambers of the *parlement* in Aix. But unlike Paris, the people of Aix were largely indifferent to the fate of the *parlement* for much of the time.

Of greater concern to the citizens of Provence was the foolish decision of the governor Louis-Emmanuel de Valois, the Count of Alais, a grandson of King Charles IX, to appoint consuls in the principal towns by letters patent in the place of locally elected representatives. The Count of Alais also annoyed the population of Aix by bringing in troops. The countryside was not much affected, but the reaction of the towns was stimulated by the happenings in Paris. On 15 January 1649 the king, regent and the cardinal fled to St-Germain. On 11 March, the Treaty of Rueil ended the first Fronde after the rebels had been forced to treat. The court returned to Paris on 18 August.

The second Fronde was led by Henri, Vicomte de Turenne, who had successfully commanded the troops that fought the Spaniards in Flanders. It was called the Fronde of the Nobles. The civil war broke out in December 1649, a reflection of the power struggle between Mazarin and Louis II, Prince of Condé, Turenne's comrade-in-arms against the Spaniards. The second Fronde leaders, except for Turenne who escaped, were imprisoned by the crown on 18 January 1650. Had they not then been arrested the crown would have totally capitulated to Condé, giving him control of the Council of State and the power to appoint governors. For tactical reasons, Mazarin had them released on 8 February 1651.

The news of the release of the princes was greeted in Provence with an explosion of joy by the supporters of the former Count of Alais, now the Duke of Angoulême, always considered in cahoots with the princes because of his royal blood.

To understand the Frondes of Provence it is necessary to follow the tergiversations in Paris. But curiously the Fronde of Provence was not overtly directed at the royal power because it had its antecedents in earlier attacks by the governor, the Count of Alais, on the rights of the *parlement*. The happenings in Paris encouraged the Aix *parlement* to raise troops, but without the support of the people of Aix. On 20 January 1649 the barricades went up in Aix, the governor was vanquished and imprisoned in his palace. He was released on 27 March, only when concessions had been made to the insurgents. In the spring and summer of 1649 the consuls were replaced. The adversaries of the governor had gained all they desired.

A second Provençal Fronde, whose members were called *'sabreurs'* and were lined up behind the disgraced governor, held Toulon, Sisteron, Tarascon, St-Tropez, the Tour-de-Bouc, Château d'If and the islands off Hyères and Antibes. Paradoxically they were opposed by the loyalist troops supported by the *parlement* and the town of Aix, called the *'canivets'*.

Factional fights continued in Brignoles, Toulon, La Ciotat, Hyères, Draguignan, Grasse, Fréjus and Montauroux.

Alais was attacked by a *parlement*-sponsored army led by the Count of Carcès, grand-seneschal and lieutenant of the king in Provence. The bloody battle of the Val on 19 June 1649 ended in the rout of the Carcès troops. Alais' troops ravaged the countryside en route to Toulon.

In Provence the nobles showed no separatism and wanted to continue French, but with respect for its former constitution. But the governor soon lost Marseilles, which on 18 March 1650 refused him entry. The citizens greeted him with musket fire and his captain of the guards was killed. After this humiliation on 18 August, he was recalled by the ministers and free elections were held in the towns.

On 17 August 1651, the regent allied with the first Fronde against Condé. On 29 March 1652 Turenne, having switched sides and leading royalist troops, beat the Frondeurs led by Condé, at Jargeau and at Etampes on 4 May, but were beaten by Condé on 7 April at Bléneau.

The absence of a governor caused Provence to fall into anarchy. The new governor, the Duke of Mercoeur, was not appointed until 8 April 1652. The impact of the Fronde outside the Midi on Provence is shown by the victory of Jargeau which, for arcane reasons, convinced the regent and Mazarin they could at last appoint a new governor for Provence and end the anarchy.

Mercoeur restored order and dispelled Frondeur sympathies in Provence, largely by distributing patronage. He seized back with royal troops Tarascon, la Tour de Bouc, Antibes, St-Tropez, St-Maximin, Brignoles, Sisteron and finally Toulon, where Alais quit on 13 September 1652. He was later arrested.

A provisional Fronde government was set up in Paris in July after fighting in the Faubourg St-Antoine; Mazarin left France and offered a general amnesty. The defection of Condé's soldiers and the increasing hostility of the bourgeoisie caused Condé to leave Paris and throw in his lot with Spain.

On 21 October, Louis XIV re-established government in Paris and recalled Mazarin. Leading Frondeurs were exiled. The surrender of Breisach of March 1654 ended the Fronde. The monarchy won out in the end and Louis XIV was crowned on 7 June. On 27 January 1660, Condé obtained in Aix-en-Provence the forgiveness of the king.

*

Louis XIV considered Marseilles a rebel city. In January 1660, the Duke of Mercoeur entered it at the head of 7,000 troops. Canons were sent to Toulon and defences broken down. The constitution was changed to leave no doubt that Marseilles was subject to the King of France. The king himself entered the city on 2 March 1660. The symbol of the submission was a gift of 50,000 livres for the king's marriage, and 40,000 livres as a bonus.

Negotiations over money continued. The success of Provence in its haggling was shown in 1671 when the king's minister Colbert pointed out that Provence was the lightest taxed province in the kingdom. However, the monarchy tightened its hold over Provence from 1671 by appointing intendants with far-reaching powers, even including the religious and cultural life. In 1752 the intendant showed his good sense when he explained before a court why he had allowed church services to be conducted in Provençal. French was the language of writing, but Provençal largely the language of speaking.

Not until 1691 did Louis XIV decide to try to seize the other major city on the Mediterranean littoral, which was Nice in the hands of Savoy.

On 12 March the French cavalry forded the Var and the infantry threw a bridge across the river. First Villefranche surrendered, followed by the forts of Montalban and St-Hospice. The citizens of Nice surrendered, but the governor of the castle, Count de Frosasque, refused. A shell fell into the dungeon of the castle and the reserve of ammunition exploded. When the count gave in, he handed over to the French a castle in complete ruin. The French seized the Haut Var, Peille, Escarène, Sospel, Breil, Saorge, La Brigue and Tende. The French occupied the whole county of Nice until the Treaty of Turin in 1696.

*

WARS OF SUCCESSION

Peace was not to last. The War of the Spanish Succession between the Grand Alliance of Britain, Holland and Austria and France started in 1701. Savoy joined on the side of France but in 1703 switched sides. On 3 March 1705, French troops again crossed the Var and seized Villefranche, La Turbie, l'Escarène and Sospel. The French navy sailed into the Nice Baie des Anges. Nice was wrecked by a fierce bombardment, eventually surrendered the town, but not the castle. There was six months' truce but the siege continued. Only in April 1706 after immense bombardment did the castle surrender. Louis XIV ordered demolition of the castle, which took five months. The fortresses of St-Hospice, La Turbie and the Beaulieu tower were also destroyed. On 21 July 1706, Nice was declared an open city.

Victor Amadeus II of Savoy was not defeated by the travails of Nice and the county. In 1707, at the head of the imperial troops, he bypassed Nice, crossed the Var and sacked Grasse. Repulsed at Toulon, pillaging in their retreat, his troops crossed back over the Var. The French followed them and reoccupied the county as far as Sospel. Out of keeping with practice of the times, in 1709 the French brought in wheat to alleviate a famine. By the Treaty of Utrecht in 1713, France recognised Victor Amadeus as King of Sicily and that he should rule Nice. France got back Barcelonnette and its valley. In 1720 the Duke swapped Sicily for Sardinia, which was nearer home. The house changed its name to Sardinia. Exhausted by the wars and all the diplomacy, in 1730 Victor Amadeus abdicated in favour of his son, Charles Emmanuel III.

Charles Emmanuel initially sided with France against Austria in the War of the Austrian Succession that started in 1740, but then, like his father, switched sides and fought the French and Spaniards from 1743. The county of Nice was once again ravaged as the two armies of France and Spain crossed the Var from their base in Antibes and seized Nice against no resistance, also Villefranche and other parts of the region. In a counter-attack in 1746, the Austro-Sardinian army not only took Nice, but crossed the Var and took possession of Villeneuve, St-Paul, Grasse and Draguignan. Only Antibes resisted. A few months later the French and Spaniards were back again, liberating the conquered towns until they got as far as Genoa. The Sardinians got back all their possessions following the Treaty of Aix-la-Chapelle in 1748.

CHAPTER NINE

Revolutions 1787–1860

THE RIVIERA'S ROLE IN REVOLUTIONS

The Riviera played an important role in the French Revolution of 1789, both in the revolution itself and in the counter-revolution.

In 1787 the Estates, which had not met since 1639, were convened in Provence and the rest of France. The Estates consisted of three orders: the clergy, nobility and commoners. The nobility had tax privileges, which they justified by claiming their contribution to the state came through the blood they shed as fighting men, a clearly outdated concept. In Provence the nobles were much more numerous than the other two orders and refused to give up their financial privileges.

The Estates met again in Provence in January and February 1789. It was argued that, rather than being an element of progress, the constitution of Provence was a tool in the hands of the privileged to oppress the third estate. The claim was that the Estates were unrepresentative because there were no parish priests in the first estate and only municipal officials in the third.

The method of representation for the countrywide Estates General was similarly disputed.

The effect on the crops of the disastrous winter of 1788–89 caused troubles to break out in many towns on the Riviera in the spring of 1789, including Marseilles, Toulon, Aups, Draguignan, La Seyne, Ollières, Le Beausset, Solliès, Hyères and Puget. The Provençal noble and politician, the Count of Mirabeau, described Provence as visited by the Exterminating Angel: *"Everywhere I have found men dead of cold and hunger, and that in the midst of wheat for lack of flour, all the mills being frozen."*

On 25 April 1789 complaints of neighbouring communes were brought together in Grasse. Antibes demanded abolition of privileges and voting by head-count. Cannes objected to the abuses of the abbot of Lérins. All attacked high taxes. The inhabitants of the county of Nice later complained about taxes, which were felt particularly acutely in an area of poor land and the ravages of earlier wars.

The proportion of communes which had clubs, which inspired the Revolution, shows the importance of the Riviera in the Revolution. Between 1791 and September 1793, 100 per cent of the districts of Toulon and Hyères had clubs and about 70 per cent in the Var as a whole. By contrast in Melun, just south of Paris, out of a total of 116 communes there were clubs in only 10 places.

'The Great Fear' was the belief that an army of court-inspired brigands was going to destroy the harvest, ransack property and starve the people into submission, which would force the self-proclaimed National Assembly to capitulate to the nobility. The imaginary sightings of the brigands were often agricultural labourers looking for work. But, starting in northern France on 20 July 1789, it caused the local populations to take up arms and destroy seigneurial titles and papers. The Great Fear swept the Riviera and reached Vence, Cannes and Antibes on 3 August.

*

FINAL ABSORPTION OF PROVENCE INTO FRANCE

On 4 August in Paris, the Estates General abolished all privileges, including those of the provinces. It was the final act of absorption of Provence into France, which had started in 1481. Provence ratified it in September 1789.

The administrative effect of the Revolution and the subsequent war was that what we know today as the Riviera, including Monaco, was carved into three departments of the Basses-Alpes, the Var and the Bouches-du-Rhône. Districts going back to the Romans were now abolished. Aix was made the capital of the Bouches-du-Rhône, but Marseilles seized that role in 1792, legally confirmed in 1800. Napoleon made Draguignan the capital of the Var in 1797, but it lost that role to Toulon in 1974.

Marseilles had its own storming of the Bastille on 2 May 1790 when it took the forts of St-Jean and St-Nicolas and massacred out in the street Major de Beausset, commandant of the St-Jean fort. It had the benefit of the counsel of the Count of Mirabeau, one of the leaders of the Revolution. In 1791–2 the Marseilles Jacobin club vigorously opposed the counter-revolutionaries in Arles and Avignon. The delegation of national guardsmen it sent to Paris in the summer of 1792 was nationally famous for the part it played in the overthrow of the monarchy.

War came again in July 1792 when Victor Amadeus of Sardinia declared his alliance with Austria against France. When the inhabitants of Nice spied the French fleet, they panicked and 20,000, including around 5,000 émigrés, fled up the road to Tende and Piedmont along with Sardinian soldiers. The French army invaded and quickly seized almost all of the county, including, on 29 September, Nice. Only the valley of the Roya, north of Sospel, stayed in the hands of the Sardinians. In response to local demand, on 31 January 1793, the county of Nice was united with France. The French army occupied Monaco, dethroned the prince and Monaco was also united with France.

In Marseilles concern with the defence of the Revolution caused a Jacobin offensive against suspect royalists. The region was in a state of turmoil. After the suppression of a royalist uprising in July 1792, some 1,500 arrests were made throughout the Midi. Four hundred men were called out to put down a disturbance in La Ciotat, a town divided by struggles between rich citizens and workless artisans. Towards the end of July, thirteen men, including the public prosecutor of the Var and members of the departmental authority, were murdered in Toulon. In September there were four lynchings. In the autumn of 1792, Marseilles sent envoys to Nice to urge them to raise themselves to the exalted revolutionary standards of the Provençal port.

The aggressiveness of the Jacobins and their clubs alienated many from the Revolution in Provence. Their downfall came in April 1793 in the face of the Sections, which were local debating assemblies in Marseilles. The counter-revolution (known as federalism) in Marseilles was in no doubt when on 27 April 1793 the deputies on mission from Paris fled the city. Leading clubists were soon arrested. On 10 June the General

Committee of Marseilles voted to establish a departmental army to crush the 'anarchists' of Paris. It would march on Paris under the slogan 'One and Indivisible Republic, respect for persons and properties'.

On 12 June, Marseilles formally declared itself 'in a legal state of resistance against oppression'. Federalist counter-revolution came to Draguignan on 4 July and soon after to Hyères, Barjols, Pierrefeu, Collobrières, Solliès and Fréjus. Toulon was infected on 12 July. Almost all the Riviera became an area of resistance to the Revolution until 1799. Exceptions were Grasse and St-Paul-de-Vence.

How could a revolution thus reverse itself? The French historian M. Vovelle, a specialist on the subject, has suggested that it was because the masses turned their animosity from the nobility to the rising bourgeoisie, whom they increasingly resented.

The attack on the Church was particularly notable in the south of France. Burlesque charivaris were popular with donkeys dressed in bishops' robes and mitres and paraded through the streets. Mannequins of the Pope would be burned. Marriage ceremonies for priests were celebrated, sometimes involuntarily.

With the port of Marseilles blockaded and the new harvest not yet in, bread riots burst out in early August 1793. The Popular Tribunal began to execute known Jacobins. Priests reappeared in public praying for divine aid to save the rebels. The monarchists of Marseilles sought an accommodation with Admiral Hood, commander of the British Mediterranean fleet, but the city fell to French government troops on 25 August before the agreement was finalised.

However, the military port of Toulon recognised Louis XVII and opened up to the British on 27 August. Paris sent the army to punish Toulon, which capitulated on 18 December and was where the young Napoleon won his spurs. Some 7,000 inhabitants fled on departing vessels. Severe punishment was meted out to those who remained and over 1,000 were executed. Toulon was stripped of its name and became 'Port-la-Montagne'. Marseilles was provisionally named 'Sans Nom'. In Marseilles the Revolutionary Tribunal, which sat between August 1793 and April 1794, tried 975 suspects of whom 240 had been born in Marseilles, 11 in the Alpes-Maritimes and 40 in the Var. The tribunal acquitted 476. A total of 289 of those convicted were executed. In the Great Terror, 412 persons were condemned to death in Marseilles.

The counter-terror continued in the Midi with anarchic murder gangs picking off selected targets implicated in Jacobinism. Corpses were dumped in front of cafés or inns or thrown in the river.

*

GUILLOTINE

The French Revolution would not have been complete in Nice without a guillotine, which arrived to meet the needs of the Alpes-Maritimes on 20 November 1793. The problem was that there was no one to execute. So Nice lent it at the beginning of December to Grasse, which was then in the Var, which executed thirty citizens. They included six priests, ten workmen, four officials, five 'bourgeois', one lawyer, one merchant, one spinster and one nun. Grasse returned it to Nice on 20 January, when they received their own machine. The Nice workmen initially refused to set up the machine, but eventually it was erected on the place d'Egalité, now the place du Palais de Justice, but without being used.

The distinguished village of Opio, which lies 5 km to the east of Grasse and which housed the summer palace of the bishops of Grasse, had the distinction of having supplied the first clerical martyr from the diocese. Its priest Ollivier was dragged from the village to a prison in Grasse. He died on his way to execution in Toulon.

Nice was not to be done out of the other fashion of the Revolution – fancy children's names. So Messidor, Septidi, Eglantine, Liberté and Sans-culotte were duly baptised.

The White Terror, which started on 4 May 1795 in Lyons, was so called because white was the royalist colour. It was most pronounced in the towns and villages of southern France. Murders took place in prisons but there were also isolated killings, beatings and other atrocities across the countryside of the south-east. Historians have estimated there were 2,000 victims.

By the Treaty of Paris of 1796, the King of Sardinia renounced to

France all his rights to the county of Nice. By the Treaty of Paris of 1814, France reverted to its frontiers of 1792 and Sardinia got back the county of Nice. France gave Monaco back to its prince.

Brigandage and confusion reigned on the Riviera until the turn of the century. The concordat between the papacy and the French government of July 1801 at last showed the inhabitants that stability was returning.

The visits of Napoleon to the Riviera in 1814 and 1815 brought it into a prominence it had not had since St Louis, King of France had landed in Hyères in 1254 on his return from the Crusades. On his 1814 visit Napoleon, who had abdicated, was on his way to Fréjus en route to his banishment on the island of Elba. The journey had its dangers in the pro-monarchy Midi and on occasion he had to disguise himself by wearing the uniform of one his allied escorts. His sister Pauline met him in Fréjus. On 28 March he sailed on the British frigate, HMS *Undaunted*.

Napoleon escaped from Elba and returned to the Riviera on 1 March 1815 on *L'Inconstant*, the ship the allies had bizarrely allowed him in his exile. On his 8 small ships were 1,142 men and 2 light cannon. They landed at Golfe-Juan and camped out on the dunes at Cannes near today's Croisette, facing an old chapel that is now the church of Notre-Dame. Early the next morning Napoleon took the road through Le Cannet to Grasse, where the mayor immediately surrendered. (By contrast the twenty men he sent to Antibes were arrested and imprisoned by the local garrison.) On through St-Vallier-de-Thiey, Escragnolles and Séranon, where he spent the night at the Château de Broundet, the country seat of the Marquis de Gourdon. The next morning he stopped for broth in Le Logis-du-Pin. Thence he was well on his way to Grenoble and eventually to Paris and his defeat at Waterloo.

To encourage tourism, the French government in 1934 established the 'Route Napoléon', which he had followed.

Antibes swung from right to left after Waterloo. Sardinian and Austrian troops tried to enter in August 1815, but the French garrison kept them out, being subject to a siege for several weeks, until the diplomacy in Paris dictated that they be let in.

Louis XVIII ruled France from 1814 to 1824, except for the interlude of Napleon's 100 days before Waterloo. Charles X reigned from 1824 to 1830, when he was succeeded by Louis Philippe who ruled until 1848. After a republican period Louis-Napoleon, Napoleon III, nephew of Bonaparte, ruled as emperor from 1852 until 1870.

CHAPTER TEN

French Nice 1860–1914

FRANCE ACQUIRES NICE AND SAVOY

Napoleon III acquired the county of Nice and Savoy from Piedmont-Sardinia on 24 March 1860, subject to a referendum, which was held the following month. According to the official figures in Nice, 25,743 were in favour and only 160 against. The Alpes-Maritimes was recreated. It included Grasse and the surrounding area, which had previously been part of the department of the Var.

The origins of the change went back to a secret meeting Napoleon III had with Count Camillo di Cavour, Prime Minister of Piedmont-Sardinia, at Plombières in the Vosges on 20 July 1858. Napoleon outlined his plans for a federally united Italy without Austria, which then held Lombardy and Venetia. The motive of Napoleon was to contain Austria. Piedmont-Sardinia could count on French support in a war. The main French reward would be the eventual acquisition of Savoy, militarily important to France. A treaty of alliance between France and Piedmont-Sardinia was signed on 19 January 1859 which provided that Nice, as well as Savoy, would be ceded to France. The idea of a federal Italy was dropped, but France would support Piedmont-Sardinia in the event of war. Cavour and Napoleon did not have to wait long for a *casus belli*. On 19 April Austria issued an ultimatum to Piedmont-Sardinia to disarm, which Cavour rejected on 26 April. On 29 April Austrian forces crossed the Piedmont-Sardinia frontier. The French declared war on 3 May and their army entered Italy. They beat the Austrians at the two famous battles of Magenta and Solferino.

Napoleon made a truce with Francis Joseph, the Austrian Emperor, at Villafranca on 11 July and Austria ceded Parma and Lombardy to France for eventual cession to Piedmont-Sardinia. Napoleon did not immediately demand from Piedmont-Sardinia his reward of Nice and Savoy because the Austrians still held Venetia. But when central Italian states moved to join the kingdom of Sardinia, Cavour offered Nice and Savoy to Napoleon, subject to a referendum, if he would accept the adhesion of the Italian states to the kingdom, which he did. Thus Nice became part of the French Riviera and the momentous return to one of the 'natural frontiers' was marked by a celebratory visit to Nice of Napoleon III and Empress Eugénie in the autumn of 1860.

On 2 February 1861, Charles III Prince of Monaco sold to France the rights he owned over Roquebrune and Menton.

Napoleon III had been indulgent to Victor-Emmanuel by letting him keep the communes of La Brigue and Tende, which had always been attached to the county of Nice, because he liked to hunt there. In 1947 Italy ceded them to France, ratified by a plebiscite, except for two small plots of land containing Mount Bego engravings.

*

TOURISM

Tourism, especially British, created the Riviera we know today. There had earlier been occasional visitors. Travel developed during the period of peace in Europe between 1763 and 1792. The principal reason was the climate. The climate of Nice, which was part of the Italian House of Savoy at the time, was supposedly curative.

There had been links between England and the House of Savoy since the sixteenth century. At the beginning of the eighteenth century, Nice was a free port for the British, therefore a small British colony existed in Nice. Henry Cavendish, the famous scientist, was born in Nice in 1731. One of the first visitors to France after travel became possible again following Britain's victory over France in the Seven Years' War was Dr Tobias Smollett MD in 1763. Smollett, ill with incipient tuberculosis, journeyed to Nice, seeking a kinder climate than England. When he returned to England he published a book of his experiences, *Travels*

Through France and Italy, which was destined to start a revolution in the travel habits of the British. The British gentry settled in the Croix de Marbre quarter of Nice, which was known as Newborough or Little London. By 1787, 110 English families stayed in Nice.

Members of the British royal family had also popularised the city. During the winter of 1784, the Duke of Cumberland, the brother of George III, with his wife and Prince William, the future William IV, and the Princess Sophie, the daughter of the king, all stayed in Nice.

Thomas Jefferson visited the Riviera in 1787 when he was Minister to France in Paris. In Nice, he stayed in the Hôtel de York from April 10 to 13 and May 1 to 2 1787. April 13 was Jefferson's forty-fourth birthday.

The building where he lodged is the old palace of the aristocratic family of Spitalieri de Sessile at 5 rue de la Préfecture, then called the place St-Dominique, and it housed the Hôtel de York. The palace was built between 1762 and 1768 and it exists today. It is a fine building, looking out on to the main square, with an elaborate wrought-iron door crowned with a balcony. Horizontal bands of stucco separate the four floors, which is characteristic of the Nice palaces of the eighteenth century.

He wrote of Nice in *Hints on European Travel* in 1788: *"I lodged at the Hotel de York. It is a fine English tavern, very agreeably situated and the mistress a friendly agreeable woman. There is another English hotel of equal reputation. The wine of Nice is remarkeably (sic) good. You may pass many days here very agreeably. It is in fact an English colony."*

The first to buy a villa on the Riviera was Lady Penelope Rivers in 1787. Her villa Furtado-Heine, a Venetian palace, situated at 121 rue de France in Nice still exists today.

The role of the British was underlined in 1834 when the outbreak of cholera in Provence led, by chance, to the establishment of Cannes as a major resort. Lord Brougham, a former Lord Chancellor of England, was on his way to Nice with his sickly daughter and on 28 December 1834 was stopped at the Sardinian frontier because of the outbreak of cholera. He stayed in the little fishing village of Cannes and was so delighted with it that he bought a piece of land and built a villa. This striking representative of early nineteenth-century Britain had no difficulty in encouraging his friends also to build there and so was founded the large British colony in Cannes.

The British always predominated, but the Russians' visits increased at a faster rate. In 1850–51 there were 189 British and 52 Russian families in Nice, but by 1856–57 the British had increased to 284 and the Russians to 141. The visits of the Russian Empress-Mother, Alexandra Feodorovna, widow of Nicholas I, with her sickly son, in 1856–57 and 1859, were important in attracting other Russians.

But the extravagant visits of Russian royalty to the Riviera were not all that they seemed. They had a political objective. The Treaty of Paris, which ended the Crimean War, excluded Russia from Europe and neutralised the Black Sea. The Russians needed a base on the Mediterranean to replace Sebastopol. They found it in Villefranche. Soon a Russian naval squadron was anchored in Villefranche harbour and the streets of Nice teemed with Russian sailors. The Sardinian government presented the cession of facilities in the port to the Russians on a lease of twenty years as purely commercial. Lord Palmerston, the British foreign minister, was not convinced. The Odessa Steamship Company, which was to exploit the facilities, according to Palmerston was *a subterfuge employed by the Russian government to evade the Treaty of Paris … When it wanted to it could transform its vessels into warships.*

In 1860, 704 foreign families spent at least part of the winter in Nice. They included 252 English, 172 French, 128 Russians, 37 Germans and 22 Americans. Other nationalities were also represented and the Queen of Denmark acquired a villa on the boulevard Carabacel.

The British predominated on the Riviera to such an extent that when the writer, Alexandre Dumas, asked an innkeeper what was the nationality of the guests who were just arriving, he said that they were all English, but he was not sure if they were Germans or Russians. The British introduced to the Riviera regattas, tennis courts (the first one appeared in Cannes in 1881), cricket, croquet, lawn tennis and golf.

The first waves of visitors either built or rented villas. But by 1847 Nice boasted thirty hotels and as they became more and more luxurious, visitors started often to prefer them to villas.

Bad or non-existent roads had always been the greatest barrier to the development of tourism on the Riviera. On the west were the mountains of the Esterel, which were difficult to cross and which also carried the risk of encounters with bandits. Once at the border with Nice, the barrier of the River Var was often overcome only by being ferried on the shoulders of the locals. The sea route had the danger of pirates. It took sixteen days of continuous and uncomfortable travel to reach Nice from London. Improvements to the roads by Napoleon for military reasons cut the journey to under two weeks early in the nineteenth century. Nice was connected to Menton and the Italian Riviera only by a mule track laid by the Romans as part of the Via Aurelia. Napoleon improved things somewhat by cutting a carriageway eastwards from Nice – the Grande Corniche.

On 10 April 1863 the railway from Paris first reached Cannes and the journey time was only twenty-one hours twenty-eight minutes. In October 1864, it reached Nice and in 1869 Menton.

The impact of the railways on the numbers of visitors who stayed in the area was considerable. At the start of the 1860s, about 4,000 visitors stayed in Nice. By 1879 the number had at least trebled to between 12,000 and 15,000. But by the end of the century the number of visits had increased six to eightfold to about 100,000.

The census for the Alpes-Maritimes of March 1886 showed 43,770 foreigners resident in the department. Ten years later the number had increased by two-thirds to 72,265. In 1886 there were only 870 English, Scottish and Irish but by 1896 the number of British had quadrupled to 3,509.

James Gordon Bennett Jr was the most famous and most eccentric American to live on the Riviera in the nineteenth century. He owned the *New York Herald* newspaper, founded the *Paris Herald,* now called the *International New York Times* and built a house in Beaulieu. But he might never have founded the Paris newspaper and come to live in Beaulieu if he had not scandalised New York society by urinating in the fireplace at a New Year's Day reception given by his fiancée's parents. It happened on 1 January 1877 and shortly thereafter he left for Paris, where he took an apartment on the Champs Elysées. He did not marry his fiancée.

Not until 8 June 1882 did the local press on the Riviera mention

Bennett's name, although it seems likely that he visited there before then. The *Phare du Littoral* reported on the coming arrival in Villefranche of *"... the largest of the yachts belonging to Mr James Gordon Bennett, manager of the New York Herald, whose luxury surpasses anything we have ever seen."* Bennett, once Commodore of the New York Yacht Club, was always known as the Commodore. He tired of sailing and built the steamship *Namouna* in Newburg, New York. It was 75 metres long, carried a crew of seventy and caused a great stir when it steamed into the bay of Villefranche on 10 February 1883.

It was on his new boat the *Sereda*, which could navigate the inland waterways, that the Commodore sailed from Paris to Beaulieu in 1886. What enticed him to Beaulieu was a restaurant, the Réserve, famous then and famous today. After lunch Bennett would take a constitutional walk round Beaulieu and fell in love with a village that a journalist of the time described as *"charming like the boudoir of a pretty woman"*. At that time it had only three hotels and a few villas occupied by foreigners. It was then part of the commune of Villefranche. The Réserve was a long way from the Beaulieu railway station. So on 17 February 1891, Bennett started a Nice-Beaulieu mail coach. It was primarily to serve the needs of the restaurant, but Bennett's initiative benefited the whole village.

Bennett's next munificence to Beaulieu in 1891 was the installation at his expense of a telephone in the Réserve so that he – and other clients – could conveniently make reservations. It was the first telephone in the area.

Bennett loved giving prizes carrying his name, some of which still exist today. They included international races for schooners, planes, balloons and cars.

The Riviera was where Bennett met his wife. She was Maud Potter, an American from Philadelphia, widow of George Julius Reuter, son of Baron Paul Julius Reuter, founder of the international news organisation. He had retired to Nice in 1878 and died at his Villa Reuter, 97 Promenade des Anglais in 1899. It is not surprising, given their common interest in news, that Bennett and Reuter should have seen much of each other on the Riviera. That Reuter-Bennett link continued after the Baron's death with a friendship between Bennett and George Julius Reuter, who died in 1909. Bennett married the widow on 10 September 1914, thus ending his many years of bachelordom. James Gordon Bennett died in Beaulieu on 14 May 1918.

The local government were very conscious of the transformation tourism had wrought on the economy of the Riviera, and Nice in particular, compared with the rest of France, as shown in the population growth. In the half century between 1861 and 1911 the population of France grew by only 5.9 per cent. The population of the Department of the Alpes-Maritimes grew by 83 per cent. But Nice, which had 44,091 inhabitants in 1861, had grown to 142,940 in 1911, an increase of 225 per cent.

Queen Victoria set an example to her citizens and the rest of Europe by visiting the Riviera nine times between 1882 and 1889, staying in Menton, Cannes, Grasse, Hyères and Nice. The most important hotel on the Riviera, the Excelsior Régina, was built with her needs in mind. (She brought 100 staff with her.) Her visits coincided with a realisation amongst the doctors of Europe that Switzerland was a better destination for tuberculosis suffers than the Riviera. So the French greatly appreciated that Queen Victoria showed that visitors should come to the Riviera not for reasons of health, but enjoyment.

Apart from tourism, the Riviera benefited in the nineteenth century from the French colonial empire in North Africa, West Africa and the Far East. The character of Marseilles changed from being largely a trading port to a centre of industry. Italian immigrants replaced the people from the interior. The continuation of such specialised activities as the perfumes of Grasse was also important. In Grasse, the activities dated from the sixteenth century when Catherine de' Medici introduced the new fashion of wearing perfumed gloves. In 1875, sixty perfumeries existed in the city.

*

MONACO

Monaco came into its own in the latter half of the nineteenth century. In 1856, Charles III of Monaco granted a concession to Napoleon Langlois and Albert Aubert to establish a sea-bathing facility for the treatment of various diseases, and to build a German-style casino in Monaco. The project did not succeed and the concession was sold to François Blanc. He had had success with a casino in Bad-Homburg in Germany and repeated it in Monaco, where he opened in 1858. The casino grew only slowly, largely due to the area's inaccessibility from much of Europe. The opening of the railway in 1868, however, brought with it an influx of people into Monte Carlo and much wealth.

CHAPTER ELEVEN

World Wars 1914–1945

SUMMER TOURISM

The most important economic development on the Riviera after World War I was the creation of the summer tourist season by the Americans. Before the Americans arrived in the 1920s, visitors came only in the winter. American GIs on 'Rest and Recreation' at the end of World War I showed the locals the pleasures of bathing in the sea and sunbathing.

The American composer Cole Porter invented the summer season on the Riviera. He and his wife rented a house on Cap d'Antibes for two summers in 1921 and 1922, inviting the wealthy Americans Gerald and Sara Murphy to stay. The Murphys then invited Scott and Zelda Fitzgerald. And thus was the new season launched. The extraordinarily wealthy Goulds put Juan-les-Pins on the map with hotels financed by American railway money.

Other personalities on the Riviera in the '20s included Edith Wharton, Isadora Duncan, Rex Ingram, Rudolph Valentino, Man Ray, Harpo Marx, Vladimir Nabokov, James Thurber, Dorothy Parker, Ernest Hemingway, Josephine Baker, Sidney Bechet, Pablo Picasso, Mary Cassatt and Coco Chanel. This was the era of the Lost Generation, the hedonistic Jazz Age, known in France as *les années folles* (the crazy years).

Anne-Elizabeth Dutheil de la Rochère, the historian of the Nice Victorine studios, said that it was Rex Ingram, the American director, who was considered in France as the creator of a mini-Hollywood. It was he who gave an international dimension to the great studios of Nice.

But it was the Lumière brothers who gave birth to the cinema on the Riviera in 1895 with *L'Arrivée d'un train en gare de La Ciotat* (*Arrival of a train in La Ciotat station*). That film laid the foundation of a French film industry, which made France the second largest exporter of films in the world after the United States.

Ingram moved to the Riviera in 1924. He rescued the bankrupt Victorine studios in Nice by arranging for their lease by MGM Studios. He later acquired the lease for himself. The studios had been founded in 1919 by Serge Sandberg and between 1919–1922, Sandberg made eight films there.

The first film Ingram made on the Riviera was *Mare Nostrum* for MGM. So impressed was the French government by the economic benefits that the making of the film at the abandoned film studios would bring to the Riviera that they lent Ingram two submarines for filming off Villefranche and Toulon. The cast was mainly European with few Americans.

The city of Nice was delighted by the employment the studios gave and by the illustrious visitors who came there. Writers included George Bernard Shaw, the Scott Fitzgeralds and John Galsworthy. Actors included Charlie Chaplin, Douglas Fairbanks, Gladys Cooper and Mary Pickford. Fairbanks claimed the Ingram Studios were the best in Europe after UFA in Berlin.

An important part of the history of cinema on the Riviera is also the story of Marcel Pagnol's studios in Marseilles, which he built between 1935–1937. There he shot *Fanny*, the third film in his famous series of characters from the old port of Marseilles.

Since the beginning of the twentieth century, far from the movies and the rich tourists, the main cities of the Riviera were socialist, part of the '*Midi Rouge*'. Marseilles became associated with the underworld, which was a hangover from the banditry rife on the Riviera in the nineteenth century. In the 1920s and '30s organised crime emerged linked to political parties, although not the communists. Its image suffered from such events as the assassination of King Alexander of Yugoslavia and the French foreign minister Louis Barthou in October 1934.

ITALY AND VICHY

World War II, which had started on 3 September 1939 when France and Britain declared war on Germany, culminated in defeat for France and the signature of an armistice with Germany on 22 June 1940. Marshal Pétain had replaced Paul Reynaud as head of the French administration based in Vichy in the centre of France on 16 June. The Germans occupied two-thirds of the country and only the southern third was administered by Vichy.

The sybaritic life of the Riviera was shattered when the Italians declared war on France and Britain on 10 June 1940 and invaded the region. They had twenty-four divisions; the French had only six. The appalling cost for Italy in the Battle of the Alps from 21 to 24 June for little gain is shown by the casualty statistics: Italian dead 631, missing 616; French dead 37. An armistice was signed on 24 June and the Italians kept the small area of only 82,217 hectares stretching from Menton to the frontier, which they had occupied. It contained only 28,000 people.

In 1882 Queen Victoria had chosen Menton as the first place she visited on the Riviera. The town erected a monument to her on 10 April 1939. The Italians threw it into the sea, but it was erected again in 1960.

The French were subject to a demilitarised zone 50 km from the Italian occupied area. The Italians established offices for the Italian Armistice Mission with France (CIAF) in a number of Riviera towns, including Marseilles and Nice. When they met in October 1940, Hitler promised Mussolini he could eventually have Nice. Italian irredentists campaigned for the return of Nice and the newspaper *Il Nizzardo* proclaimed its rallying cry as *"Nizza fino alla morte"* (Nice until death). The Italians refused to allow French schools to reopen but opened nine Italian schools.

By the beginning of World War II more than one-quarter of the population of the French departments bordering Italy were either Italians or of Italian heritage. The Italian CIAF missions were inundated by complaints about the French from these Italians. The Nice commission received complaints about noise at night from French neighbours, a dog urinating against a fence and unpaid rent. Tension was rampant between the two nationalities. Following an anti-foreigner Vichy law of 17 July

1940, all Italians working at a municipal level in the Alpes-Maritimes were laid off. The Italians had missed a trick by not writing into the armistice a veto on such legislation. However, French officials in leftist municipalities like Grasse and St-Laurent-du-Var were also fired.

Not surprisingly, officials on the Riviera sent sycophantic messages to Marshal Pétain when he became the head of the Vichy government. Pétain owned a country house in Villeneuve-Loubet in the Alpes-Maritimes and the mayors of the nearby villages got permission to name the area *La Vallée du Maréchal*. However, the feeling of the general public is better shown by its behaviour when the James Stewart film *Mr Smith Goes to Washington* was screened. Whenever liberty was mentioned the audience applauded. On 14 July 1942 there was an open demonstration in the centre of Nice by several hundred young people chanting, "Long Live de Gaulle" and "Death to Laval and Hitler".

Attitudes were partly conditioned by food shortages, not helped by the severe droughts in 1942 and 1943. Protests by housewives were significant. A quite subtle form of dissent was to carry two fishing rods: *'deux gaules'*. More obvious propaganda was important, ranging from 'V' for Victory signs and posters to pamphlets and newspapers.

When the Allies invaded North Africa on 8 November 1942, the Germans moved into the unoccupied Vichy zone and the Italian army expanded its occupation zone to include all Provence to the River Rhône, except for Marseilles, which the Germans took. There were German enclaves in Toulon, Cuers, Hyères and St-Raphael.

The Italian invasion by 150,000 soldiers verged on comedy, with whole units losing their way, partly because of faulty guidance by French locals. It took up to ten days for some units to get from Menton to Grasse and Cannes. German tardiness meant that the French fleet in Toulon was able to scuttle seventy-seven ships on 27 November 1942 to prevent the Germans from using the French fleet against the Allies.

A curiosity of this period is the mixed nature of the rule. The prefect of the Alpes-Maritimes, Marcel Ribière, wrote to the department's mayors on 16 November 1942: *"You are not occupied. The Italian troops are not occupation troops but operational troops. The sovereignty of the French authorities is integrally preserved."*

Attacks on the Italian troops started on 27 April 1943 when three officers were gunned down in Nice and one died. The attacks continued spasmodically until the Italian troop withdrawal.

The first the Italian commander knew about the Allies and Italy signing an armistice was on 8 September 1943 when he heard it on the Allied radio. There was occasional resistance from the disbanded Italian troops. The small Italian garrison in the Nice railway station refused to surrender and entered into hand-to-hand fighting with the Germans in a last-ditch stand. At least 62,000 Italian soldiers ended up in German prison camps.

*

RESISTANCE

The Riviera was one of the leaders of the Resistance in France. With its socialist and communist background, Marseilles was a fulcrum. Within weeks of the signature of the armistice between France and Germany, Henri Frenay from Marseilles was distributing his *Manifeste* and recruiting demobilised soldiers from the armistice army. Marseilles was a centre for secret service agents, escaped prisoners, French and foreign anti-Nazis, Alsations, Christian-Democrats, Masons and Jews.

The total number of Jews deported from the Alpes-Maritimes was 3,164, of which only 121 returned. A total of 782 Jews were seized in the big round-up in the old port of Marseilles in August 1943, when nearly 6,000 people were arrested and 1,642 sent to concentration camps. However, the Italian army made great efforts to protect Jews.

Antibes and Cannes were veritable turntables with so many British agents arriving and leaving. When the Riviera Resistance got going with sabotage it made its mark between 30 April and 10 November 1942, with twenty-three explosive attacks. But there was a firm policy *"to avoid premature large-scale rising of patriots"*.

The French Milice was formed to support the occupying forces in January 1943. In February the law defining the *Service du Travail*

Obligatoire (Compulsory Labour Service) – *STO* – was enacted to oblige certain categories of men to register for work in Germany. The consequence was that many fled to the countryside to join the Resistance, which in that region was largely made up of rural bands of guerrilla fighters – the Maquis.

General de Lattre de Tassigny commented on the Maquis: *"One will never say often enough how many thousands and thousands of dead the Maquis have saved us in the landings in Provence. General Eisenhower said the Resistance had been worth fifteen divisions."*

However, some less senior officers did not agree. *"Resistance is small business,"* said Macdonald Austin, an officer of the American Office of Strategic Services (OSS). It was the moral contribution of the secret war that was beyond price.

The term 'Maquis' was well established when de Lattre paid his tribute on 16 August 1944. But it had only come into use in the first half of 1943.

Jean Moulin was the prefect of the department of Eure et Loire at the beginning of the war. Marshal Pétain sacked him on 2 November 1940 as *"partisan of the ancien régime."* He settled in the Bouches-du-Rhône under a pseudonym. On a quiet Saturday afternoon in 1940 he had slipped into the sub-prefecture in Grasse and filched a rubber stamp for an exit permit. Moulin managed to leave France on 9 September 1941 and made his way to London, where in October he met de Gaulle. De Gaulle gave him wide powers and named him his personal representative in the Vichy zone. His code name initially was Rex and later Max.

An art gallery in Nice played an important role in Moulin's Resistance activities. He opened a gallery called *La galérie Romanin* in Nice as his front. The *vernissage* in February 1943 was attended not only by prominent members of the French administrations in Nice, but also by the Germans. The first shows included works by Utrillo, Marie Laurencin, Dufy and Matisse. Henri Manhès, a resister, provided him with a discreetly placed apartment in the town. The first radio message he sent to London was from a pension near Bargemon in the Var.

Moulin returned to London from 13 February to 21 March 1943. De Gaulle made him his sole representative for all France with the title of

President of the Future National Council of the Resistance *(CNR)*.

Moulin was betrayed to the Gestapo at a Resistance meeting in a doctor's surgery in the Caluire suburb of Lyons on 21 June 1943 and, after torture, died in Metz on 8 July.

Moulin's task had been to knit together the often-feuding Resistance groups, riven with political in-fighting for their positions on Liberation. On the Riviera the main groups were:

FTP or *FTPF, francs-tireurs et partisans:* armed communist resistance, part of the *Front National (FN)*. The *FN* was the movement of resistance of the French Communist Party. In 1944, it was intent on starting a national insurrection. In that year the *FTP* was unified with other paramilitary groups.

Libération, also known as *Libération-sud:* the leading left-wing southern resistance group, anti-Nazi, with syndicalists and socialists.

Combat: the largest non-communist organisation. Its Riviera headquarters were in Marseilles. Marseilles was also important as the headquarters of the Pat O'Leary line which saved Allied airmen who had been shot down.

Franc-tireur: Centre-left southern resistance group, non-communist.

A coordinating committee was set up for the southern zone on 27 November 1942, followed on 26 January 1943 by the *Mouvement Unis de Résistance (MUR)*. The *MUR* was created by Jean Moulin to unify *Combat, Libération-sud* and *Franc-tireur*. In April the *MUR* established a *Service National du Maquis (SNM)*. Moulin achieved non-communist unity for the whole of France on 27 May 1943 with the first meeting in Paris of the *Conseil National de la Résistance (CNR)*. It eventually included the communists. At the end of the year all the resistance movements and networks from both zones were unified in the *Mouvement de Libération Nationale (MLN)*. The *Armée Secrète (AS)*, the military arm of the *MUR*, was theoretically separate from the Maquis, but from the end of 1943 and the beginning of February 1944 all armed resistance was merged into the *Forces Françaises de l'Intérieur (FFI)*.

The most common attacks by the Resistance were communications – telephone cables and railways. But if we were to seek to identify the most important of the attacks on the Riviera it was probably the repeated destruction at great danger to the attackers of the bauxite factory of Barras in Marseilles, which produced the aluminium essential for aircraft production. Also important was a strike by workers at the metallurgical factories in Marseilles and attacks in Toulon.

When General Eisenhower announced on 8 September 1943 that the Italians had signed an armistice with the Allies, there was dancing in the streets of Nice. But the next day at dawn the Germans invaded the area between the Var and the Italian frontier, which was the part of the Italian sector they had not already seized. By then the Var was standing out as the Riviera department with the greatest food supply problems. Dissent in Mediterranean areas increased following the decision of the Germans in mid-January 1944 to evacuate the coastal strips to facilitate construction of military defences.

Statistics on the Resistance and related issues are still much debated, partly because of the problem of definition. Should those who read Resistance newspapers and those who helped the Resistance be included as members of the Resistance? Examples are gendarmes who closed their eyes to Resistance activities; those who occasionally delivered packages; those who hid Jews. One estimate says less than 2 per cent of the population of France – at most 500,000 – were involved in the Resistance. Another puts it at a million. Up to 100,000 are thought to have died – executed, killed in combat or dying in the camps. One historian gives a figure of 24,000 fighting on the Riviera. Estimates of the number of identity cards issued to fighters in 1944 range from 230,000 to 300,000.

Robert O. Paxton, one of the leading authorities on the Resistance, considers the most official number (those awarded the coveted post-war *Carte de combatant volontaire de la Résistance* that entitled one to veterans' benefits), which was 262,730 as of 2008, was too low because it included few civil resisters and almost no women. He says:

> *At the other extreme, if we count those who read the approximately 1,200 clandestine newspapers, we find a broader circle of several million sympathisers willing to take some risks. If one defines authentic resistance as including some degree of illegal activity, as one must, the best estimates lie between 300,000 and 500,000 active resisters.*

Italian repression in the south-east of France was relatively modest compared with the German. Forty Frenchmen were killed by the Italians and 875 deported, of which 34 did not return. In the Alpes-Maritimes, the Germans executed 159 resisters and deported 397, of which 177 did not return. In the Var, the Germans executed 140 and deported 341.

Despite its many losses the Riviera was spared a major massacre, such as at Oradour-sur-Glane near Limoges where 642 men, women and children were machine-gunned, asphyxiated or burned alive. But the Riviera suffered a great blow in July 1943 when the leadership of the *MUR* in Marseilles, Toulon and Nice was decapitated in the *Flora* affair, when many were betrayed.

The village of Signes in the Var has no less than three memorials to the fifty-eight resisters executed by the Germans in 1944.

*

THE CHAMPAGNE CAMPAIGN

The invasion of the South of France by the Allies in August 1944 was preceded by a softening-up bombardment. Between 28 April and 10 August 1944 the Allies flew more than 10,000 sorties over the Riviera and dropped 12,500 tons of bombs. The most devastating incident was the bombardment of St-Roch in Nice, where 280 were killed and 100 went missing. In the five days after 10 August before they landed on 15 August, the Allies dropped 5,000 tons of bombs. Most of the population were taking shelter from Allied bombing in cellars without food, water or light for almost a week before the invasion.

The landing, which was originally called Anvil and later Dragoon, was from Cap Nègre in the west and Théoule-sur-Mer in the east. The US Navy historian Samuel Eliot Morison said the landings were *an example of an almost perfect amphibious operation from the point of view of training, timing, Army-Navy-Air Force cooperation, performance, and results.* However, views differed on the benefits of the 'Champagne Campaign' (officially known as 'Dragoon') on the two major Allied campaigns in western Europe – the invasion of northern France and the fighting in Italy. As the official military history of the campaign said: *"Supporters, mainly American, pointed out its vital assistance to the former, and detractors, mostly British, emphasised its pernicious influence on the latter."*

Some Americans had reservations about the British contribution: *"When I first landed I came across two dead British soldiers lying by a big equipment bundle. When we opened it up to see what they had been after, we found that the damned thing was about 50 pounds of tea. Nothing else. That's what these guys had been after when they were killed."*

The Americans and the Canadians in the 7th Army bore the brunt of the invasion, but the French forces under General de Lattre de Tassigny played an important role, shown by the masterly decision of de Lattre simultaneously to attack Toulon and Marseilles. French intelligence was vital, exemplified in the final survey of the landing areas by a French OSS agent bicycling from Cannes to Hyères on August 13. De Lattre commented on the superb intelligence he got from the Resistance.

Before the arrival of the liberating forces there were uprisings in Marseilles, Toulon, Nice and Draguignan.

The main thrust of the invasion was up the Rhône valley towards the north. The Germans did little to fight for the Riviera itself, mainly confining themselves to laying mines and blowing up bridges. The 1st Airborne Task Force, which had been dropped inland near Draguignan, was joined by the 1st Special Service Forces, which had liberated the islands off Hyères, and they swept across the Riviera along the coast and also inland to the Italian border over a period of three weeks.

The invasion was not all plain sailing. A notable error due to communication problems was that British paratroopers due to land near Le Muy in the Var landed 30 km away near Tourrettes and Fayence. However, the area was soon liberated.

The Resistance played an important role in the capture of Cannes. Colonel Schneider had orders to destroy the city before he evacuated it. But he left the hotels and civic structures intact, perhaps as a result of a deal with the Resistance. When Schneider reached Nice he was court-martialled for dereliction of duty and executed.

The mixture of a giddy social life and fighting was reminiscent of the ball the Duke of Richmond held on 15 June 1815, three days before the Battle of Waterloo. After Nice fell on 30 August, the Allies faced tough German opposition to their attempt to get into Italy to the east – but it did not deter them from enjoying the nightlife of the Riviera. One sergeant-major described the contrasts:

> *Nice was an exciting place for youngsters like ourselves. It was full of entertainment of all kinds. Some of the finest hotels and restaurants in the world are there and every one of them seemed to be willing to put themselves at our service in exchange for the supplies we carried.*
>
> *There was also excitement in the fact that we could go out on patrol during the day, maybe getting into a little fire fight, perhaps getting all bloody and muddy in the process, then five hours later be sitting in one of the biggest night clubs in the world with a babe and a bottle of champagne.*

One of the reasons the troops were so relaxed was that the Ultra decrypts from the listening post at Bletchley Park in England told them that the Germans planned no counter-attack.

As in the period at the end of and after World War I, the Riviera was most notable as a 'Rest and Relaxation Area' (USRRA) for American troops. Hotels were requisitioned and at one point 40,000 soldiers and 12,000 officers were arriving each week. By December 1945 no fewer than 350,000 American troops had vacationed there. Most of the soldiers were in Nice, but the officers were in Cannes and Juan-les-Pins. The atmosphere was relaxed and notices were put up: USRRA: no saluting by restees required in this area. A number of GIs married French girls. But there were also conflicts between the French and Americans. One soldier got twenty years' hard labour for an attack on the mayor of Nice.

The so called 'purification' which followed the occupation of the Riviera by the Allied troops was particularly intense in Marseilles, where there was much torturing and many executions. Of the eighty-eight deaths in the Alpes-Maritimes during the purification, no less than thirty-seven occurred in Nice. Cannes had only five, Antibes three and Grasse and Vence one each.

Monaco was neutral during the war, but so eager was Prince Louis to dissociate the principality from the French and so impressed had he been by the Americans that he requested the United States to annex Monaco as American territory. The Minister of State made the request to Major-General Robert Frederick, the general commanding the Riviera coastline and the Italian border. The general recovered from the shock and told him that such an annexation was no function of the military and that he should make such a representation through the State Department.

CHAPTER TWELVE

Peace 1945

PAINS OF RECONSTRUCTION

On 10 November 1947, after the victory of the Rally of the French People (RPF Gaullist) in the municipal election in October, a vast movement of insurrectional strikes that shook France for several months started in Marseilles, protesting against tram fare increases.

Four strikers were charged following the demonstrations. To free them, 4,000 demonstrators entered the courthouse, and then went to the city hall. They insulted and defenestrated the Gaullist lawyer Michel Carlini, who had become alderman by defeating by one vote the communist Jean Cristofol. The protesters then attacked shady bars near the opera. The young communist worker Vincent Voulant was killed by the Mafia clan Guerini.

In Toulon on 4 December there were incidents at the tramway depot and in Antibes, an attack on the post office.

*

ALGERIA

The next major political event which especially affected the Riviera was Algerian independence.

Between March and May 1962, 200,000 people left Algeria, most of them with only suitcases. In June, 350,000 landed in France, mostly in Marseilles. After the vote on independence of Algeria in July, the exodus grew again. At the end of the year 650,000 had left Algeria for good and had been resettled, mostly in the south of France. Despite being banned from the departments that had become saturated with refugees in July 1962 (the Bouches-du-Rhône, the Alpes-Maritimes, the Var and Vaucluse), at the beginning of 1963, 60 per cent of the refugees were in the southern departments or in the Paris region. Thus, 50 per cent of the urban development of the city of Marseilles, and many other cities, was attributable to the refugees.

Renowned for the strength of the communists immediately post-war, the Riviera soon slipped more and more to the right.

Industries that were particularly active post-war were entertainment, tourism and technology.

*

CANNES FILMS

One of the first events to take place on the Riviera as France shook off the agonies of war was the Cannes Film Festival. It owed its origins to Italian fascism. The Venice Film Festival was founded in 1932, but in 1938, although Jean Renoir's *La Grande Illusion* was tipped to win top prize it went to *Olympia*, produced in association with the Nazi Ministry of Propaganda in Berlin, and *Luciano Serra, pilota*, made by the son of the Fascist leader Benito Mussolini. The French were outraged and withdrew from the competition in protest. Both the British and American members of the jury resigned.

A French diplomat, Philippe Erlanger, who had been sent to Venice by the French government was appalled by the prize given to *Olympia*. With the Minister of Education and Fine Arts, Jean Zay, he determined to launch a concurrent festival to show that France, as a democracy, had a great cinema too. He was the first delegate of the festival. Not only the Riviera towns of Nice, Monaco and Cannes competed for the business, but also Biarritz and Vichy, Aix-les-Bains and Le Touquet. Cannes won because of its 'sunny and enchanting location' and the French government tried to launch the first festival there in September 1939. But it had to be abandoned because of the outbreak of World War

II. In 2002 nonetheless, a 'Jury 1939' gave awards to films and actors from the selection of 1939. On 20 September 1946 the first Cannes Film Festival proper was launched. In later years, it was staged in May to avoid competition with Venice, It was an American, Grace Moore, who opened the festival by singing the *Marseillaise* with a choir from Antibes.

The participation of the Americans was of course important for the festival, but in terms of the top prizes they did not initially dominate. The top prize was originally called the *Grand Prix du Festival International du Film* and later the *Palme d'Or*. The *Palme d'Or* was introduced in 1955 and was won by the American film *Marty*, directed by Delbert Mann. In the first ten years of the festival the Americans won three (14 per cent), of the twenty-one top prizes awarded, which was the same number as France and Italy. In the first thirty years the US won only eight of the forty-two prizes (17 per cent), which was less than Italy with ten (21 per cent). Only later did Hollywood eventually dominate and in the next twenty-five years, won eight more of the twenty-nine prizes awarded (27 per cent).

Along the coast at St-Tropez, a new personality burst onto the scene: Brigitte Bardot. The 1956 film *Et Dieu … créa la femme* (in which she starred) put St-Tropez on the map and drew tourists in droves. *Le Gendarme de Saint-Tropez,* opening with the song Do you, do you, do you Saint-Tropez gave the town another publicity triumph in 1964.

*

JAZZ

The success of the Cannes Film Festival inspired the idea of a jazz festival.

Older inhabitants of the Riviera would have had a sense of déjà-vu on 2 June 1945 when eighty-six musicians of the US Army Band played for 30,000 Niçois dancing in the place Masséna in celebration of victory in World War II.

Nice launched the first jazz festival on the Riviera, or indeed in the world, from 22 to 28 June 1948, at the end of the carnival.

The famous Sidney Bechet got back to France in 1949, this time for the Paris Jazz Festival. In 1950 he went down to Juan-les-Pins to play at the Riviera version of the Paris Vieux Colombier nightclub; the beginning of a long love affair with Juan-les-Pins, where he played every year until his death in 1959. It was on the Riviera in 1951 that he made his biggest impact when he married in Antibes a German, Elizabeth Ziegler. Thousands turned out to cheer the wedding procession from the place Nationale to the town hall in Antibes and then on to the Vieux Colombier nightclub in Juan-les-Pins. (Juan-les-Pins lies to the west of the larger and older town of the adjoining Antibes of which it is administratively a part.) Scores of doves were released as the couple left the town hall. The procession of floats and jazz bands was half a mile long and included a 12-foot model of a soprano saxophone carried by two attendants. Thirteen gallons of rum were dispensed to warm up the crowd. So memorable was that wedding that Bechet's statue has pride of place in Juan-les-Pins.

The Riviera had to wait another ten years after the first Nice festival before it had another jazz festival. This time it was the turn of Cannes from 8 to 13 July 1958. A small town like Cannes had to share the cost, so it was combined with one in Knokke-le-Zoute on the Belgian coast and Newport in the United States.

In 1960, a year after the death of Sidney Bechet, Antibes-Juan-les-Pins held their first festival. It took place in a sports stadium below the castle of Antibes and only next year moved to the La Pinède arena in Juan-les-Pins, which seated 4,000. The festival continued year by year until 1971, when the municipality lost heart and for two years Nice took over.

On the seafront of Juan-les-Pins are embedded in cement handprints of great jazz musicians, including Claude Luter, Fats Waller and Little Richard.

Josephine Baker, who had been in the Resistance, the greatest American jazz singer and dancer the Riviera ever saw, is buried on the Riviera in the cemetery in Monaco. From her arrival in Paris in 1925 to her death there fifty years later, Josephine periodically visited the Riviera to perform or to rest. But she settled there in 1969 when Princess Grace of Monaco arranged for her to live in a house in Roquebrune-Cap-Martin, on the

Mediterranean near the Italian border with her twelve adopted children.

All these activities made the Riviera the second region for tourism in France after Paris.

*

TECHNOLOGY

Sophia-Antipolis is the business park of the Riviera. When Pierre Laffitte, the founder, first put forward the idea for such a park in an article in *Le Monde* in August 1960 he knew that the Stanford Research Park had been established in Palo Alto, California in 1953. The park and the expansion to the south became known as Silicon Valley.

Laffitte's father-in-law, Emile Hugues, Mayor of Vence, had already been instrumental in 1959 in the establishment of International Business Machines (IBM) in the nearby village of La Gaude.

A foundation was set up in 1972 to launch a business park named Sophia-Antipolis on the plain of Valbonne north of Cannes and the first companies, which were predominantly American, settled there in 1974.

Jacques Médecin, the notorious Mayor of Nice, contributed to the success of the park. In 1976 when Americans were under attack in Beirut in the Lebanon, he flew there to encourage companies to transfer their Mediterranean headquarters to the Riviera.

Under suspicion of corruption, he fled France in 1990, but was extradited from Uruguay back to France in 1993, convicted and jailed. Médecin returned to Uruguay following his release from prison. He died in Uruguay, in November 1998.

In 1991 eight companies founded the Telecom Valley Association to promote the telecommunications industry in the area. Of those eight charter members, five were American.

Thus Americans created a new relationship with the Riviera, two centuries after Thomas Jefferson had revealed its charms.

Chronology

BC
600   Greeks found Marseilles
121   Romans found Provincia Transalpina
49   Julius Caesar seizes Marseilles

AD
341   Franks invade Gaul
410   Monastery of Lérins founded
476   End of Western Roman Empire
481   Clovis becomes king of the Franks
508   Ostrogoths seize much of Provence
536   Ostrogoths cede Provence to Franks
800   Charlemagne crowned Holy Roman Emperor
843   Treaty of Verdun divides Charlemagne's empire
879   Boso elected king of Provence
1112 Barcelonan rule
1246 Angevin rule
1348 Plague
1388 Nice elects to join Savoy
1481 Provence united with France
1562 Wars of Religion
1648 Fronde breaks out
1789 Revolution
1792 Napoleon seizes Nice
1814 Nice returns to Sardinia
1860 Nice united with France
1940 Vichy government rules south of France
1942 Italians and Germans invade south of France
1944 Allies invade

1945   World War II ends
1974   Sophia-Antipolis founded

Selected Bibliography

Adleman, Robert H. and George Walton. *The Champagne Campaign: The Spectacular Airborne Invasion That Turned the Tide of the Battle in Southern France in 1944.* Boston, Mass: Little, Brown, 1969.

Beard, Mary. *SPQR: A History of Ancient Rome.* London: Profile, 2015.

Bradbury, Jim. *The Capetians: Kings of France 987–1328.* London: Continuum, 2007.

Braudel, Fernand. *The Mediterranean and the Mediterranean World in the Age of Philip II.* London: William Collins, 1972.

Cleere, Henry. *Southern France: An Oxford Archaeological Guide.* Oxford: OUP, 2001.

Cobb, Matthew. *The Resistance: The French Fight Against the Nazis.* London: Simon & Schuster, 2009.

Cunliffe, Barry. *Greeks, Romans and Barbarians.* London: Guild Publishing, 1988.

Doyle, William. *The Oxford History of the French Revolution.* Oxford: OUP, 1989.

Dunbabin, Jean. *France in the Making 843–1180.* Oxford: OUP, 2000.

Edwards, Anne. *The Grimaldis of Monaco.* New York: William Morrow, 1992.

Fenby, Jonathan. *The History of Modern France: From the Revolution to the Present Day.* London: Simon & Schuster, 2015.

Funk, Arthur Layton. *Hidden Ally: The French Resistance, Special Operations, and the Landings in Southern France, 1944.* Contributions in Military Studies. New York, London: Greenwood Press, 1992.

Goldstone, Nancy. *Joanna: The Notorious Queen of Naples, Jerusalem and Sicily.* London: Weidenfeld & Nicolson, 2010.

——. *The Rival Queens: Catherine De' Medici, Her Daughter Marguerite De Valois, and the Betrayal That Ignited a Kingdom.* London: Weidenfeld & Nicolson, 2015.

Goldsworthy, Adrian Keith. *Augustus: From Revolutionary to Emperor.* London: Weidenfeld & Nicolson, 2014.

Hale, Julian. *The French Riviera: A Cultural History.* Oxford: Signal Books, 2009.

Hodge, A. Trevor. *Ancient Greek France.* London: Duckworth, 1998.

James, Edward. *The Franks.* Oxford: Basil Blackwell, 1988.

Jones, Ted. *The French Riviera: A Literary Guide for Travellers.* London: IB Tauris, 2004.

MacKendrick, Paul. *Roman France.* New York: St Martin's Press, 1972.

Marnham, Patrick. *The Death of Jean Moulin: Biography of a Ghost.* London: John Murray, 1999.

Miller, Peter N. *Peiresc's Mediterranean World.* Cambridge, Mass: Harvard University Press, 2015.

Naphy, William G., and Andrew Spicer. *The Black Death and the History of Plagues 1345–1730.* Stroud: Tempus, 2000.

Nelson, Michael. *Americans and the Making of the Riviera.* Jefferson, NC: McFarland, 2008.

——. *Queen Victoria and the Discovery of the Riviera.* London: IB Tauris, 2001.

Price, Munro. *The Fall of the French Monarchy: Louis XVI, Marie Antoinette and the Baron de Breteuil.* London: Macmillan, 2002.

Ranum, Orest. *The Fronde: A French Revolution, 1648–1652.* New York, London: W.W. Norton, 1993.

Rivet, A.L.F. *Gallia Narbonensis: Southern Gaul in Roman Times.* London: Batsford, 1988.

Smollet, Tobias. *Travels Through France and Italy.* Fontwell: Centaur Press, 1969.

Tuchman, Barbara W. *A Distant Mirror: The Calamitous 14th Century.* London: Macmillan, 1979.

Woolf, Greg. *Becoming Roman: The Origins of Provincial Civilization in Gaul.* Cambridge: CUP, 1998.

Acknowledgements

This book would not have been possible without the help of those listed below:

Marcus Bicknell, chairman, Clarence Bicknell Association; Marilyn Bowler, senior development associate, Magdalen College, Oxford; Philippe Boudoux, deputy director, Institut Français, London; François Croquette, director, Institut Français, London; Robert Elphick, former Reuter journalist; Jonathan Fenby, author of *The History of Modern France: From the Revolution to the Present Day;* Steven Gunn, Professor of Early Modern History, Oxford University; Rachel Mazuy, Associate Researcher, CNRS, Paris; Helga Nelson; Patrick Nelson, designer; David Parrott, Associate Professor of Modern History, Oxford University; Christopher Phipps, Indexer; Munro Price, Professor of Modern European History, Bradford University; Olivier Rauch, proviseur, Lycée français Charles de Gaulle, London; Silvia Sandrone, responsable scientifique et documentaire, Musée des Merveilles, Tende; Amanda Scott, director of development, Latymer Foundation; Stephen Somerville, former Reuter journalist; David Ure, former Reuter executive; Lin Wolff, owner of the English Book Centre, Valbonne, France, who suggested I write the book.

Index

CPSIA information can be obtained
at www.ICGtesting.com
Printed in the USA
FSOW04n2002280217
31398FS